CURSE OF THE STARVING CLASS

A PLAY IN THREE ACTS
BY **SAM SHEPARD**

★

★

DRAMATISTS
PLAY SERVICE
INC.

CURSE OF THE STARVING CLASS
Copyright © 1976, Sam Shepard

All Rights Reserved

SPECIAL NOTE

CAST

(in order of appearance)

WESLEY	Ebbe Roe Smith
ELLA	Olympia Dukakis
EMMA	Pamela Reed
TAYLOR	Kenneth Welsh
WESTON	James Gammon
ELLIS	Eddie Jones
MALCOLM	John Aquino
EMERSON	Michael J. Pollard
SLATER	Raymond J. Barry

Original New York Production by New York Shakespeare Festival Presented by Joseph Papp

Directed by Robert Woodruff

ACT 1

SCENE:

Upstage center is a very plain breakfast table with a red oilcloth covering it. Four mismatched metal chairs are set one at each side of the table. Suspended in midair to stage right and stage left are two ruffled, red-checked curtains, slightly faded. In the down left corner of the stage are a working refrigerator and a small gas stove, set right up next to each other. In the down right corner is a pile of wooden debris, torn screen, etc., which are the remains of a broken door. Lights come up on WESLEY, *in sweatshirt, jeans and cowboy boots, who is picking up the pieces of the door and throwing them methodically into an old wheelbarrow. This goes on for a while. Then* WESLEY's *mother,* ELLA, *enters slowly from down left. She is a small woman wearing a bathrobe, pink fuzzy slippers, hair in curlers. She is just waking up and winds an alarm clock in her hand as she watches* WESLEY *sleepily.* WESLEY *keeps cleaning up the debris, ignoring her.*

ELLA: *(after a while)* You shouldn't be doing that.

WESLEY: I'm doing it.

ELLA: Yes, but you shouldn't be. He should be doing it. He's the one who broke it down.

WESLEY: He's not here.

ELLA: He's not back yet?

WESLEY: Nope.

ELLA: Well, just leave it until he gets back.

WESLEY: In the meantime we gotta' live in it.

ELLA: He'll be back. He can clean it up then.

WESLEY goes on clearing the debris into the wheelbarrow. ELLA *finishes winding the clock and then sets it on the stove.*

ELLA: *(looking at clock)* I must've got to sleep at five in the morning.

WESLEY: Did you call the cops?

ELLA: Last night?

WESLEY: Yeah.

ELLA: Sure I called the cops. Are you kidding? I was in danger of my life. I was being threatened.

WESLEY: He wasn't threatening you.

ELLA: Are you kidding me? He broke the door down didn't he?

WESLEY: He was just trying to get in.

ELLA: That's no way to get into a house. There's plenty of other ways to get into a house. He could've climbed through a window.

WESLEY: He was drunk.

ELLA: That's not my problem.

WESLEY: You locked the door.

ELLA: Sure I locked the door. I told him I was going to lock the door. I told him the next time that happened I was locking the door and he could sleep in a hotel.

WESLEY: Is that where he is now?

ELLA: How should I know?

WESLEY: He took the Packard I guess.

ELLA: If that's the one that's missing I guess that's the one he took.

WESLEY: How come you called the cops?

ELLA: I was scared.

WESLEY: You thought he was going to kill you?

ELLA: I thought— I thought, "I don't know who this is. I don't know who this is trying to break in here. Who is this? It could be anyone."

WESLEY: I heard you screaming at each other.

ELLA: Yes.

WESLEY: So you must've known who it was.

ELLA: I wasn't sure. That was the frightening part. I could smell him right through the door.

WESLEY: He was drinking that much?

ELLA: Not that. His skin.

WESLEY: Oh.

ELLA: *(suddenly cheerful)* You want some breakfast?

WESLEY: No, thanks.

ELLA: *(going to refrigerator)* Well I'm going to have some.

WESLEY: *(still cleaning)* It's humiliating to have the cops come to your own house. Makes me feel like we're someone else.

ELLA: *(looking in refrigerator)* There's no eggs but there's bacon and bread.

WESLEY: Makes me feel lonely. Like we're in trouble or something.

ELLA: *(still looking in refrigerator)* We're not in trouble. He's in trouble, but we're not.

WESLEY: You didn't have to call the cops.

ELLA: *(slamming refrigerator door and holding bacon and bread)* I told you, he was trying to kill me!

They look at each other for a moment. ELLA *breaks it by putting the bacon and bread down on top of the stove.* WESLEY *goes back to cleaning up the debris. He keeps talking as* ELLA *looks through the lower drawers of the stove and pulls out a frying pan. She lights one of the burners on the stove and starts cooking the bacon.*

WESLEY: *(as he throws wood into wheelbarrow)* I was lying there on my back. I could smell the avocado blossoms. I could hear the coyotes. I could hear stock cars squeeling down the street. I could feel myself in my bed in my room in this house in this town in this state in this country. I could feel this country close like it was part of my bones. I could feel the presence of all the people outside, at night, in the dark. Even sleeping people I could feel. Even all the sleeping animals. Dogs. Peacocks. Bulls. Even tractors sitting in the wetness, waiting for the sun to come up. I was looking straight up at the ceiling at all my model airplanes hanging by all their thin metal wires. Floating. Swaying very quietly like they were being blown by someone's breath. Cobwebs moving with them. Dust laying on their wings. Decals peeling off their wings. My P-39. My Messerschmitt. My Jap Zero. I could feel myself lying far below them on my bed like I was on the ocean and overhead they were on reconnaissance. Scouting me. Floating. Taking pictures of the enemy. Me, the enemy. I could feel the space around me like a big, black world. I listened like an animal. My listening was afraid. Afraid of sound. Tense. Like any second something could invade me. Some foreigner. Something undescribable. Then I heard the Packard coming up the hill. From a mile off I could tell it was the Packard by the sound of the valves. The lifters have a sound like nothing else. Then I could picture my Dad driving it. Shifting unconsciously. Downshifting into second for the last pull up the hill. I could feel the headlights closing in. Cutting through the orchard. I could see the trees being lit one after the other by the lights, then going back to black. My heart was pounding. Just from my Dad coming back. Then I heard him pull the brake. Lights go off. Key's turned off. Then a long silence. Him just sitting in the car. Just sitting. I picture him just sitting. What's he doing? Just sitting. Waiting to get out. Why's he waiting to get out? He's plastered and can't move. He's plastered and doesn't want to move. He's going to sleep there all night. He's slept there before. He's woken up with dew on the hood before. Freezing headache. Teeth covered with peanuts. Then I hear the door of the Packard open. A pop of metal. Dogs barking down the road. Door slams. Feet. Paper bag being tucked under one arm. Paper bag covering "Tiger Rose" Feet coming. Feet walking toward the door. Feet stopping. Heart pounding. Sound of door not opening. Foot kicking door. Man's voice. Dad's voice. Dad calling Mom. No answer. Foot kicking. Foot kicking harder. Wood splitting. Man's voice. In the night. Foot kicking hard through door. One foot right through door. Bottle crashing. Glass breaking. Fist through door. Man cursing. Man going insane. Feet and hands tearing. Head smashing. Man yelling. Shoulder smashing. Whole body crashing. Woman screaming. Mom screaming. Mom screaming for police. Man throwing wood. Man throwing up. Mom calling cops. Dad crashing away. Back down driveway. Car door slamming. Ignition grinding. Wheels screaming. First gear grinding. Wheels screaming off down hill. Packard disappearing. Sound disappearing. No sound. No sight. Planes still hanging. Heart still pounding. No sound. Mom crying soft. Soft crying. Then no sound. Then softly crying. Then moving around through house. Then no moving. Then crying softly. Then stopping. Then, far off the freeway could be heard.

WESLEY *picks up one end of the wheelbarrow. He makes the sound of a car and pushes it off right, leaving* ELLA *alone at the stove watching the bacon. She speaks alone.*

ELLA: Now I know the first thing you'll think is that you've hurt yourself. That's only natural. You'll think that something drastic has gone wrong with your insides and that's why you're bleeding. That's only a natural reaction. But I want you to know the truth. I want you to know all the facts before you go off and pick up a lot of lies. Now, the first thing is that you should never go swimming when that happens. It can cause you to bleed to death. The water draws it out of you.

WESLEY'*s sister,* EMMA, *enters from right. She is younger and dressed in a white and green 4-H Club uniform. She carries several hand-painted charts on the correct way to cut up a frying chicken. She sets the charts down on the table upstage and arranges them as* ELLA *talks to her as though she's just continuing the conversation.*

EMMA: But what if I'm invited? The Thompson's have a new heated pool. You should see it, Ma. They even got blue lights around it at night. It's really beautiful. Like a fancy hotel.

ELLA: *(tending to the bacon)* I said no swimming and that's what I meant! This thing is no joke. Your whole life is changing. You don't want to live in ignorance do you?

EMMA: No, Ma.

ELLA: All right then. The next thing is sanitary napkins. You don't want to buy them out of any old machine in any old gas station bathroom. I know they say "sanitized" on the package but they're a far cry from "sanitized." They're filthy in fact. They've been sitting around in those places for months. You don't know whose quarters go into those machines. Those quarters carry germs. Those innocent looking silver quarters with Washington's head staring straight ahead. His handsome jaw jutting out. Spewing germs all over those napkins.

EMMA: *(still arranging charts)* How come they call them napkins?

ELLA: *(stopping for a second)* What?

EMMA: How come they call them napkins?

ELLA: *(back to the bacon)* Well, I don't know. I didn't make it up. Somebody called them napkins a long time ago and it just stuck.

EMMA: "Sanitary napkins."

ELLA: Yes.

EMMA: It's a funny sound. Like a hospital or something.

ELLA: Well that's what they should be like, but unfortunately they're not. They're not hospital clean that's for sure. And you should know that anything you stick up in there should be absolutely hospital clean.

EMMA: Stick up in where?

ELLA *turns upstage toward* EMMA, *then changes the subject.*

ELLA: What are those things?

EMMA: They're for my demonstration.

ELLA: What demonstration?

EMMA: How to cut up a frying chicken.

ELLA: *(back to bacon)* Oh.

EMMA: For 4-H. You know. I'm giving a demonstration at the fair. I told you before. I hope you haven't used up my last chicken.

EMMA *goes to refrigerator and looks inside for a chicken.*

ELLA: I forgot you were doing that. I thought that wasn't for months yet.

EMMA: I told you it was this month. The fair's always this month. Every year it's this month.

ELLA: I forgot.

EMMA: Where's my chicken?

ELLA: *(innocently)* What chicken?

EMMA: I had a fryer in here all ready to go. I killed it and dressed it and everything!

ELLA: It's not in there. All we got is bacon and bread.

EMMA: I just stuck it in here yesterday, Ma! You didn't use it did you?

ELLA: Why would I use it?

EMMA: For soup or something.

ELLA: Why would I use a fryer for soup. Don't be ridiculous.

ELLA: *(slamming refrigerator)* It's not in there!

ELLA: Don't start screaming in here! Go outside and scream if you're going to scream!

> EMMA *storms off stage right.* ELLA *takes the bacon off the stove. Slight pause, then* EMMA *can be heard yelling off stage.* ELLA *puts some bread in the frying pan and starts frying it.*

EMMA'S VOICE: *(off)* That was my chicken and you fucking boiled it! YOU BOILED MY CHICKEN! I RAISED THAT CHICKEN FROM THE INCUBATOR TO THE GRAVE AND YOU BOILED IT LIKE IT WAS ANY OLD FROZEN HUNK OF FLESH! YOU USED IT WITH NO CONSIDERATION FOR THE LABOR INVOLVED! I HAD TO FEED THAT CHICKEN CRUSHED CORN EVERY MORNING FOR A YEAR! I HAD TO CHANGE ITS WATER! I HAD TO KILL IT WITH AN AX! I HAD TO SPILL ITS GUTS OUT! I HAD TO PLUCK EVERY FEATHER ON ITS BODY! I HAD TO DO ALL THAT WORK SO THAT YOU COULD TAKE IT AND BOIL IT!

> WESLEY *enters from left and crosses to center.*

WESLEY: What's all the screaming?

ELLA: Somebody stole her chicken.

WESLEY: Stole it?

ELLA: Boiled it.

WESLEY: You boiled it.

ELLA: I didn't know it was hers.

WESLEY: Did it have her name on it?

ELLA: No, of course not.

WESLEY: Then she's got nothing to scream about. *(yelling off stage)* SHUT UP OUT THERE! YOU SHOULD'VE PUT YOUR NAME ON IT IF YOU DIDN'T WANT ANYBODY TO BOIL IT!

EMMA'S VOICE: *(off)* EAT MY SOCKS!

WESLEY: *(crossing up to table)* Great language. *(noticing charts on table)* What's all this stuff?

ELLA: Her charts. She's giving a demonstration.

WESLEY: *(holding one of the charts up)* A demonstration? On what?

ELLA: How to cut up a chicken. What else.

ELLA takes her bacon and bread on a plate and crosses up to ·table. She sits at the stage left end.

WESLEY: Anybody knows how to cut up a chicken.

ELLA: Well, there's special bones you have to crack. Special ways of doing it evidently.

WESLEY: *(turning downstage with chart held out in front of him)* What's so special about it.

ELLA: *(eating at table)* The anatomy is what's special. The anatomy of a chicken. If you know the anatomy you're half-way home.

WESLEY: *(facing front, laying chart down on floor)* It's just bones.

EMMA'S VOICE: *(off)* THERE'S NO CONSIDERATION! IF I'D COME ACROSS A CHICKEN IN THE FREEZER I WOULD'VE ASKED SOMEONE FIRST BEFORE I BOILED IT!

ELLA: *(yelling, still eating)* NOT IF YOU WERE STARVING!

WESLEY unzips his fly, takes out his pecker, and starts pissing all over the chart on the floor. ELLA just keeps eating at the table, not noticing.

EMMA'S VOICE: *(off)* NO ONE'S STARVING IN THIS HOUSE! YOU'RE FEEDING YOUR FACE RIGHT NOW!

ELLA: So what!

EMMA'S VOICE: *(off)* SO NO ONE'S STARVING! WE DON'T BE-LONG TO THE STARVING CLASS!

ELLA: Don't speak unless you know what you're speaking about! There's no such thing as a starving class!

EMMA'S VOICE: *(off)* THERE IS SO! THERE'S A STARVING CLASS OF PEOPLE, AND WE'RE NOT PART OF IT!

ELLA: WE'RE HUNGRY, AND THAT'S STARVING ENOUGH FOR ME!

EMMA'S VOICE: *(off)* YOU'RE A SPOILED BRAT!

ELLA: *(to WESLEY)* Did you hear what she called me? *(she notices what he's doing, she yells to Emma)* EMMA!

EMMA'S VOICE: *(off)* WHAT!

ELLA: YOUR BROTHER'S PISSING ALL OVER YOUR CHARTS!
goes back to eating)

11

EMMA *enters fast from right and watches* WESLEY *put his joint back in his pants and zip up. They stare at each other as* ELLA *goes on eating at the table.*

EMMA: What kind of a family is this?

ELLA: *(not looking up)* I tried to stop him but he wouldn't listen.

EMMA: *(to* WESLEY*)* Do you know how long I worked on those charts? I had to do research. I went to the library. I took out books. I spent hours.

WESLEY: It's a stupid thing to spend your time on.

EMMA: I'm leaving this house! *(she exits right)*

ELLA: *(calling after her but staying at table)* YOU'RE TOO YOUNG! *(to* WESLEY*)* She's too young to leave. It's ridiculous. I can't say I blame her but she's way too young. She's only just now having her first period.

WESLEY: *(crossing to refrigerator)* Swell.

ELLA: Well, you don't know what it's like. It's very tough. You don't have to make things worse for her.

WESLEY: *(opening refrigerator and staring into it)* I'm not. I'm opening up new possibilities for her. Now she'll have to do something else. It could change her whole direction in life. She'll look back and remember the day her brother pissed all over her charts and see that day as a turning point in her life.

ELLA: How do you figure?

WESLEY: Well, she's already decided to leave home. That's a beginning.

ELLA: *(standing abruptly)* She's too young to leave! And get out of that refrigerator!

She crosses to refrigerator and slams the door shut. WESLEY *crosses up to the table and sits at the stage right end.*

ELLA: You're always in the refrigerator!

WESLEY: I'm hungry.

ELLA: How can you be hungry all the time? We're not poor. We're not rich but we're not poor.

WESLEY: What are we then?

ELLA: *(crossing back to table and sitting opposite* WESLEY*)* We're somewhere in between. *(pause as* ELLA *starts to eat again;* WESLEY *watches her)* We're going to be rich though.

WESLEY: What do you mean?

ELLA: We're going to have some money real soon.

WESLEY: What're you talking about?

ELLA: Never mind. You just wait though. You'll be very surprised.

WESLEY: I thought Dad got fired.

ELLA: He did. This has nothing to do with your father.

WESLEY: Well, you're not working are you?

ELLA: Just never mind. I'll let you know when the time comes. And then we'll get out of this place, once and for all.

WESLEY: Where are we going?

ELLA: Europe maybe. Wouldn't you like to go to Europe?

WESLEY: No.

ELLA: Why not?

WESLEY: What's in Europe?

ELLA: They have everything in Europe. High art. Paintings. Castles. Buildings. Fancy food.

WESLEY: They got all that here.

ELLA: Why aren't you sensitive like your Grandfather was? I always thought you were just like him, but you're not, are you?

WESLEY: No.

ELLA: Why aren't you? You're circumcized just like him. It's almost identical in fact.

WESLEY: How do you know?

ELLA: I looked. I looked at them both and I could see the similarity.

WESLEY: He's dead.

ELLA: When he was alive is when I looked. Don't be ridiculous.

WESLEY: What'd you sneak into his room or something?

ELLA: We lived in a small house.

EMMA'S VOICE: (off) WHERE'S MY JODHPURS!

ELLA: (to WESLEY) What's she yelling about?

WESLEY: Her jodhpurs.

ELLA: (yelling to EMMA) What do you need your jodhpurs for?

EMMA'S VOICE: (off) I'M TAKING THE HORSE!

ELLA: DON'T BE RIDICULOUS! DO YOU KNOW HOW FAR YOU'LL GET ON THAT HORSE? NOT VERY FAR!

EMMA'S VOICE: (off) FAR ENOUGH!

ELLA: YOU'RE NOT TAKING THE HORSE! (to WESLEY) Go down and lock that horse in the stall.

WESLEY: Let her go.

ELLA: On a horse? Are you crazy? She'll get killed on the freeway.

WESLEY: She won't take him on the freeway.

ELLA: That horse spooks at its own shadow. *(yelling off to* EMMA*)* EMMA, YOU'RE NOT TAKING THAT HORSE! *(no answer from* EMMA*)* EMMA! *(to* WESLEY*)* Go see if she went down there. I don't want her taking off on that horse. It's dangerous.

WESLEY: She's a good rider.

ELLA: I don't care!

WESLEY: You go down there then.

> *Pause. She looks at him.*

ELLA: Well, maybe she'll be all right.

WESLEY: Sure she will. She's been out on overnight trail rides before.

ELLA: What a temper she's got.

WESLEY: She's just spoiled.

ELLA: No, she's not. I never gave her a thing extra. Nothing. Bare minimums. That's all.

WESLEY: The old man spoils her.

ELLA: He's never around. How could he spoil her?

WESLEY: When he's around he spoils her.

ELLA: That horse is a killer. I wish you'd go down there and check.

WESLEY: She can handle him.

ELLA: I've seen that horse get a new set of shoes and he's an idiot! They have to throw him down every time.

WESLEY: Look, where's this money coming from?

ELLA: What money?

WESLEY: This money that's going to make us rich.

ELLA: I'm selling the house.

> *Long pause, as* WESLEY *stares at her. She turns away from him.*

ELLA: I'm selling the house, the land, the orchard, the tractor, the stock. Everything. It all goes.

WESLEY: It's not yours.

ELLA: It's mine as much as his!

WESLEY: You're not telling him?

ELLA: No! I'm not telling him and I shouldn't have told you. So just keep it under your hat.

WESLEY: How can you sell the house? It's not legal even.

ELLA: I signed the deed, same as him. We both signed it.

WESLEY: Then he has to co-sign the sale. Fifty-fifty.

ELLA: I already checked with a lawyer, and it's legal.

WESLEY: What about the mortgages? It's not even paid off, and you've borrowed money on it.

ELLA: Don't start questioning me! I've gone through all the arrangements already.

WESLEY: With who!

ELLA: I HAVE A LAWYER FRIEND!

WESLEY: A lawyer friend?

ELLA: Yes. He's very successful. He's handling everything for me.

WESLEY: You hired a lawyer?

ELLA: I told you, he's a friend. He's doing it as a favor.

WESLEY: You're not paying him?

ELLA: He's taking a percentage. A small percentage.

WESLEY: And you're just going to split with the money without telling anybody?

ELLA: I told you. That's enough. You could come with me.

WESLEY: This is where I live.

ELLA: Some home. It doesn't even have a front door now. Rain's going to pour right through here.

WESLEY: You won't even make enough to take a trip to San Diego off this house. It's infested with termites.

ELLA: This land is valuable. Everybody wants a good lot these days.

WESLEY: A lot?

ELLA: This is wonderful property for development. Do you know what land is selling for these days? Have you got any idea?

WESLEY: No.

ELLA: A lot. Tons. Thousands and thousands are being spent every day by ordinary people just on this very thing. Banks are loaning money right and left. Small family loans. People are building. Everyone wants a piece of land. It's the only sure investment. It can never depreciate like a car or a washing machine. Land will double its value in ten years. In less than that. Land is going up every day.

WESLEY: You're crazy.

ELLA: Why? For not being a sucker? Who takes care of this place?

WESLEY: Me!

ELLA: Ha! Are you kidding? What do you do? Feed a few sheep. Disc the orchard once in a while. Irrigate. What else?

WESLEY: I take care of it.

ELLA: I'm not talking about maintenance. I'm talking about fixing it up. Making it look like somebody lives here. Do you do that?

WESLEY: Somebody does live here!

15

ELLA: Who! Not your father!

WESLEY: He works on it. He does the watering.

ELLA: When he can stand up. How often is that? He comes in here and passes out on the floor for three days then disappears for a week. You call that work? I can't run this place by myself.

WESLEY: Nobody's asking you to!

ELLA: Nobody's asking me period! I'm selling it, and that's all there is to it!

Long pause, as they sit there. WESLEY *gets up fast.*

ELLA: Where are you going?

WESLEY: I'm gonna' feed the sheep!

He exits left. ELLA *calls after him.*

ELLA: Check on Emma for me would you, Wesley? I don't like her being down there all alone. That horse is crazy.

WESLEY'S VOICE: *(off)* HE'S GOING TO KILL YOU WHEN HE FINDS OUT!

ELLA: *(standing, shouting off)* HE'S NOT GOING TO FIND OUT! *(pause, as she waits for a reply; nothing; she yells again)* THE ONLY PERSON HE'S GOING TO KILL IS HIMSELF!

Another pause, as she stands there waiting for WESLEY *to reply. Nothing. She turns to the table and stares at the plate. She picks up the plate and carries it to the stove. She sets it on the stove. She stares at the stove. She turns toward refrigerator and looks at it. She crosses to refrigerator and opens it. She looks inside.*

ELLA: Nothing.

She closes refrigerator door. She stares at refrigerator. She talks to herself.

ELLA: He's not going to kill me. I have every right to sell. Every right. He doesn't have a leg to stand on.

She stares at refrigerator, then opens it again and looks inside. EMMA *enters from right, holding a rope halter in one hand, her white uniform covered in mud. She watches* ELLA *staring into refrigerator.*

EMMA: That bastard almost killed me.

ELLA *shuts refrigerator and turns toward* EMMA.

ELLA: What happened to you?

EMMA: He dragged me clear across the corral.

ELLA: I told you not to play around with that fool horse. He's insane, that horse.

EMMA: How am I ever going to get out of here?

ELLA: You're not going to get out of here. You're too young. Now go and change your clothes.

EMMA: I'm not too young to have babies, right?

ELLA: What do you mean?

EMMA: That's what bleeding is, right? That's what bleeding's for.

ELLA: Don't talk silly, and go change your uniform.

EMMA: This is the only one I've got.

ELLA: Well, change into something else then.

EMMA: I can't stay here forever.

ELLA: Nobody's staying here forever. We're all leaving.

EMMA: We are?

ELLA: Yes. We're going to Europe.

EMMA: Who is?

ELLA: All of us.

EMMA: Pop too?

ELLA: No. Probably not.

EMMA: How come? He'd like it in Europe wouldn't he?

ELLA: I don't know.

EMMA: You mean just you, me, and Wes are going to Europe? That sounds awful.

ELLA: Why? What's so awful about that? It could be a vacation.

EMMA: It'd be the same as it is here.

ELLA: No, it wouldn't! We'd be in Europe. A whole new place.

EMMA: But we'd all be the same people.

ELLA: What's the matter with you? Why do you say things like that?

EMMA: Well, we would be.

ELLA: I do my best to try to make things right. To try to change things. To bring a little adventure into our lives and you go and reduce the whole thing to smithereens.

EMMA: We don't have any money to go to Europe anyway.

ELLA: Go change your clothes!

EMMA: No. *(she crosses to table and sits stage right end)*

ELLA: If your father was here you'd go change your clothes.

EMMA: He's not.

ELLA: Why can't you just cooperate?

EMMA: Because it's deadly. It leads to dying.

ELLA: You're not old enough to talk like that.

EMMA: I was down there in the mud being dragged along.

ELLA: It's your own fault. I told you not to go down there.

EMMA: Suddenly everything changed. I wasn't the same person anymore. I was just a hunk of meat tied to a big animal. Being pulled.

ELLA: Maybe you'll understand the danger now.

EMMA: I had the whole trip planned out in my head. I was going to head for Baja California.

ELLA: Mexico?

EMMA: I was going to work on fishing boats. Deep sea fishing. Helping businessmen haul in huge swordfish and barracuda. I was going to work my way along the coast, stopping at all the little towns, speaking Spanish. I was going to learn to be a mechanic and work on four-wheel-drive vehicles that broke down. Transmissions. I could've learned to fix anything. Then I'd learn how to be a short-order cook and write novels on the side. In the kitchen. Kitchen novels. Then I'd get published and disappear into the heart of Mexico. Just like that guy.

ELLA: What guy?

EMMA: That guy who wrote *Treasure of Sierra Madre*.

ELLA: When did you see that?

EMMA: He had initials for a name. And he disappeared. Nobody knew where to send his royalties. He escaped.

ELLA: Snap out of it, Emma. You don't have that kind of a background to do jobs like that. That's not for you, that stuff. You can do beautiful embroidery; why do you want to be a mechanic?

EMMA: I like cars. I like travel. I like the idea of people breaking down and I'm the only one who can help them get on the road again. It would be like being a magician. Just open up the hood and cast your magic spell.

ELLA: What are you dreaming for?

EMMA: I'm not dreaming now. I was dreaming then. Right up to the point when I got the halter on. Then as soon as he took off I stopped. I stopped dreaming and saw myself being dragged through the mud.

ELLA: Go change your clothes.

EMMA: Stop saying that over and over as though by saying it you relieve yourself of responsibility.

ELLA: I can't even follow the way you talk to me anymore.

EMMA: That's good.

ELLA: Why is that good?

EMMA: Because if you could then that would mean that you understood me.

Pause. ELLA *turns and opens the refrigerator again and stares into it.*

EMMA: Hungry?

ELLA: No.

EMMA: Just habit?

ELLA: What?

EMMA: Opening and closing?

ELLA *closes refrigerator and turns toward* EMMA.

ELLA: Christ, Emma, what am I going to do with you?

EMMA: Let me go.

ELLA: *(after pause)* You're too young.

ELLA *exits left.* EMMA *stays sitting at table. She looks around the space, then gets up slowly and crosses to the refrigerator. She pauses in front of it, then opens the door slowly and looks in. She speaks into refrigerator.*

EMMA: Hello? Anything in there? We're not broke you know, so you don't have to hide! I don't know where the money goes to but we're not broke! We're not part of the starving class!

TAYLOR, *the lawyer, enters from down right and watches* EMMA *as she speaks into refrigerator. He is dressed in a smart suit, middle-aged, with a briefcase. He just stands there watching her.*

EMMA: *(into refrigerator)* Any corn muffins in there? Hello! Any produce? Any rutabagas? Any root vegetables? Nothing? It's all right. You don't have to be ashamed. I've had worse. I've had to take my lunch to school wrapped up in a Weber's bread wrapper. That's the worst. Worse than no lunch. So don't feel bad! You'll get some company before you know it! You'll get some little eggs tucked into your sides and some yellow margarine tucked into your little drawers and some frozen chicken tucked into your— *(pauses)* You haven't seen my chicken have you? You motherfucker!

She slams the door to refrigerator and turns around. She sees TAYLOR *standing there. They stare at each other.* TAYLOR *smiles.*

TAYLOR: Your mother home?

EMMA: I don't know.

TAYLOR: I saw her car out there so I thought she might be.

EMMA: That's not her car.

TAYLOR: Oh. I thought it was.

EMMA: It's my Dad's car.

19

TAYLOR: She drives it, doesn't she?

EMMA: He bought it.

TAYLOR: Oh. I see.

EMMA: It's a Kaiser-Fraser.

TAYLOR: Oh.

EMMA: He goes in for odd-ball cars. He's got a Packard, too.

TAYLOR: I see.

EMMA: Says they're the only ones made out of steel.

TAYLOR: Oh.

EMMA: He totaled that car but you'd never know it.

TAYLOR: The Packard?

EMMA: No, the other one.

TAYLOR: I see.

EMMA: Who are you anyway?

TAYLOR: My name's Taylor. I'm your mother's lawyer.

EMMA: Is she in trouble or something?

TAYLOR: No. Not at all.

EMMA: Then what are you doing here?

TAYLOR: Well, I've got some business with your mother.

EMMA: You're creepy.

TAYLOR: Oh, really?

EMMA: Yeah, really. You give me the creeps. There's something about
you that's weird.

TAYLOR: Well, I did come to speak to your mother.

EMMA: I know, but you're speaking to me now.

TAYLOR: Yes. *(pause, as he looks around awkwardly)* Did someone
break your door down?

EMMA: My Dad.

TAYLOR: Accident?

EMMA: No, he did it on purpose. He was pissed off.

TAYLOR: I see. He must have a terrible temper.

EMMA: What do you want?

TAYLOR: I told you—

EMMA: Yeah, but what do you want my mother for?

TAYLOR: We have some business.

EMMA: She's not a business woman. She's terrible at business.

TAYLOR: Why is that?

EMMA: She's a sucker. She'll believe anything.

TAYLOR: She seems level-headed enough to me.

EMMA: Depends on what you're using her for.

Pause, as TAYLOR *looks at her.*

TAYLOR: You don't have to be insulting.

EMMA: I got nothing to lose.

TAYLOR: You *are* her daughter, aren't you?

EMMA: What line of business are you in?

TAYLOR: Do you mind if I sit down?

EMMA: I don't mind. My Dad might mind, though.

TAYLOR: He's not home, is he?

EMMA: He might come home any second now.

TAYLOR: *(crossing to chair at table)* Well, I'll just wait for your mother.

EMMA: He's got a terrible temper. He almost killed one guy he caught her with.

TAYLOR: *(sitting in stage right chair)* You misunderstand me. I'm here on business.

EMMA: A short fuse they call it. Runs in the family. His father was just like him. And his father before him. Wesley is just like Pop, too. Like liquid dynamite.

TAYLOR: *(setting attaché case on table)* Liquid dynamite?

EMMA: Yeah. What's that stuff called?

TAYLOR: I don't know.

EMMA: It's chemical. It's the same thing that makes him drink. Something in the blood. Hereditary. Highly explosive.

TAYLOR: Sounds dangerous.

EMMA: Yeah.

TAYLOR: Don't you get afraid living in an environment like this?

EMMA: No. The fear lies with the ones who carry the stuff in their blood, not the ones who don't. I don't have it in me.

TAYLOR: I see.

EMMA: Nitroglycerine. That's what it's called. Nitroglycerine.

TAYLOR: What do you mean?

EMMA: In the blood. Nitroglycerine.

TAYLOR: Do you think you could call your mother for me?

EMMA: *(yelling but looking straight at* TAYLOR*)* MOM!!!!

TAYLOR: *(after pause)* Thank you.

EMMA: What do you want my mother for?

TAYLOR: *(getting irritated)* I've already told you!

EMMA: Does she bleed?

TAYLOR: What?

EMMA: You know. Does she have blood coming out of her?

TAYLOR: I don't think I want to talk any more.

EMMA: All right.

    EMMA *crosses to table and sits opposite* TAYLOR *at the stage left end. She stares at him. They sit silently for a while.* TAYLOR *squirms nervously, taps on his attaché case.* EMMA *just watches him.*

TAYLOR: Marvelous house this is. *(pause, as she just looks at him)* The location I mean. The land is full of potential. *(pause)* Of course it's a shame to see agriculture being slowly pushed into the background in deference to low-cost housing, but that's simply a product of the times we live in. There's simply more people on the planet these days. That's all there is to it. Simple mathematics. More people demand more shelter. More shelter demands more land. It's an equation. We have to provide for the people some way. The new people. We're lucky to live in a country where that provision is possible. In some countries, like India for instance, it's simply not possible. People live under banana leaves.

    WESLEY *enters from right carrying a small collapsible fence structure. He sets it up center stage to form a small rectangular enclosure. He turns and looks at* TAYLOR, *then turns to* EMMA.

WESLEY: *(to* EMMA*)* Who's he?

EMMA: He's a lawyer.

    TAYLOR *stands, smiling broadly at* WESLEY *and extending his hand.* WESLEY *doesn't shake but just looks at him.*

TAYLOR: Taylor. You must be the son.

WESLEY: Yeah, I'm the son.

    WESLEY *exits right.* TAYLOR *sits down again. He smiles nervously at* EMMA, *who just stares at him.*

TAYLOR: It's a funny sensation.

EMMA: What?

TAYLOR: I feel like I'm on enemy territory.

EMMA: You are.

TAYLOR: I haven't felt this way since the war.

EMMA: What war?

TAYLOR *just looks at her.* WESLEY *enters again from right carrying a small live lamb. He sets the lamb down inside the fenced area. He watches the lamb as it moves around inside the fence.*

EMMA: *(to* WESLEY*)* What's the matter with him?

WESLEY: *(watching lamb)* Maggots.

EMMA: Can't you keep him outside? He'll spread germs in here.

WESLEY: *(watching lamb)* You picked that up from Mom.

EMMA: Picked what up?

WESLEY: Germs. The idea of germs. Invisible germs mysteriously floating around in the air. Anything's a potential carrier.

TAYLOR: *(to* WESLEY*)* Well, it does seem that if the animal has maggots it shouldn't be in the kitchen. Near the food.

WESLEY: We haven't got any food.

TAYLOR: Oh. Well, when you do have food you prepare it in here, don't you?

EMMA: That's nothing. My brother pisses on the floor in here.

TAYLOR: Do you always talk this way to strangers?

EMMA: Look, that's his piss right there on the floor. Right on my chart.

WESLEY: *(turning to* TAYLOR*)* What're you doing here anyway?

TAYLOR: I don't feel I have to keep justifying myself all the time. I'm here to meet your mother.

WESLEY: Are you the one who's trying to sell the house?

TAYLOR: We're negotiating, yes.

EMMA: *(standing)* What? Trying to sell what house? This house?

TAYLOR: *(to* EMMA*)* Didn't she tell you?

WESLEY: She told me.

EMMA: Where are we going to live!

WESLEY: *(to* EMMA*)* You're leaving home anyway. What do you care?

EMMA: *(yelling off stage)* MOM!!!

TAYLOR: *(to* WESLEY*)* I didn't mean to shock her or anything.

WESLEY: *(to* TAYLOR*)* Aren't you going to talk to my old man.

TAYLOR: That's not necessary right now.

WESLEY: He'll never sell you know.

TAYLOR: Well, he may have to. According to your mother he owes a great deal of money.

EMMA: To who? Who does he owe money to?

TAYLOR: To everyone. He's in hock up to his ears.

EMMA: He doesn't owe a cent! Everything's paid for!

WESLEY: Emma, shut up! Go change your clothes.

EMMA: You shut up! This guy's a creep, and he's trying to sell us all down the river. He's a total meatball!

WESLEY: I know he's a meatball! Just shut up, will you?

EMMA: *(to TAYLOR)* My Dad doesn't owe money to anyone!

TAYLOR: *(to WESLEY)* I'm really sorry. I thought your mother told her.

ELLA enters from left in a dress and handbag with white gloves. TAYLOR stands when he sees her.

ELLA: What's all the shouting going on for? Oh, Mr. Taylor. I wasn't expecting you for another half-hour.

TAYLOR: Yes, I know. I saw the car out in front so I thought I'd stop in early.

ELLA: Well, I'm glad you did. Did you meet everyone?

TAYLOR: Yes, I did.

ELLA: *(noticing lamb)* What's that animal doing in here, Wesley?

WESLEY: It's got maggots.

ELLA: Well, get him out of the kitchen.

WESLEY: It's the warmest part of the house.

ELLA: Get him out!

EMMA: Mom, are you selling this house?

ELLA: Who told her?

TAYLOR: Well, I'm afraid it slipped out.

ELLA: Emma, I'm not going to discuss it now. Go change your clothes.

EMMA: *(coldly)* If you sell this house, I'm never going to see you again.

EMMA exits left. TAYLOR smiles, embarrassed.

TAYLOR: I'm very sorry. I assumed that she knew.

ELLA: It doesn't matter. She's leaving anyway. Now, Wes, I'm going out with Mr. Taylor for a little lunch and to discuss our business. When I come back I want that lamb out of the kitchen.

TAYLOR: *(to WESLEY, extending his hand again)* It was very nice to have met you.

WESLEY ignores the gesture and just stares at him.

ELLA: *(to TAYLOR)* He's sullen by nature. Picks it up from his father.

TAYLOR: I see. *(to WESLEY)* Nitroglycerin, too, I suppose? *(chuckles)*

ELLA and TAYLOR start to exit off right. ELLA turns to WESLEY.

ELLA: Keep an eye out for Emma, Wes. She's got the curse. You know what that's like for a girl, the first time around.

TAYLOR and ELLA exit. WESLEY stands there for a while. He turns and looks at the lamb.

WESLEY: *(staring at lamb)* "Eat American Lamb. Twenty million coyotes can't be wrong."

He crosses to refrigerator and opens it. He stares into it.

WESLEY: You're out of luck. Santa Claus hasn't come yet.

He slams refrigerator door and turns to lamb. He stares at lamb.

WESLEY: *(to lamb)* You're lucky I'm not really starving. You're lucky this is a civilized household. You're lucky it's not Korea and the rains are pouring through the cardboard walls and you're tied to a log in the mud and you're drenched to the bone and you're skinny and starving, but it makes no difference because someone's starving more than you. Someone's hungry. And his hunger takes him outside with a knife and slits your throat and eats you raw. His hunger eats you, and you're starving.

Loud crash of garbage cans being knocked over off stage right. Sound of WESTON, WESLEY's father, off right.

WESTON'S VOICE: *(off right)* WHO PUT THE GODDAMN GARBAGE CANS RIGHT IN FRONT OF THE GODDAMN DOOR?

WESLEY listens for a second, then bolts off stage left. More crashing is heard off right. General cursing from WESTON, then he enters from right with a large duffel bag full of laundry and a large bag full of groceries. He's a very big man, middle-aged, wearing a dark overcoat which looks like it's been slept in, a blue baseball cap, baggy pants, and tennis shoes. He's unshaven and slightly drunk. He takes a few steps and stops cold when he sees the lamb. He just stares at the lamb for a minute, then crosses to the table and sets the bag of groceries and the laundry on the table. He crosses back to center and looks at the lamb inside the fence.

WESTON: *(to Lamb)* What in the hell are you doin' in here? *(he looks around the space, to himself)* Is this inside or outside? This is inside, right? This is the inside of the house. Even with the door out it's still the inside. *(to lamb)* Right? *(to himself)* Right. *(to lamb)* So what the hell are you doing in here if this is the inside? *(he chuckles to himself)* That's not funny.

He crosses to the refrigerator and opens it.

WESTON: Perfect! ZERO! ABSOLUTELY ZERO! NADA! GOOSE EGGS! *(he yells at the house in general)* WE'VE DONE IT AGAIN! WE'VE GONE AND LEFT EVERYTHING UP TO THE OLD MAN AGAIN! ALL THE UPKEEP! THE MAINTENANCE! PERFECT!

He slams the refrigerator door and crosses back to the table.

25

WESTON: I don't even know why we keep a refrigerator in this house. All it's good for is slamming.

He picks up the bag of groceries and crosses back to the refrigerator, talking to himself.

WESTON: Slams all day long and through the night. SLAM! SLAM! SLAM! What's everybody hoping for, a miracle! IS EVERYBODY HOPING FOR A MIRACLE?

He opens refrigerator as WESLEY *enters from stage right and stops.* WESTON's *back is to him.* WESTON *starts taking artichokes out of the bag and putting them in the refrigerator.*

WESTON: *(to house)* THERE'S NO MORE MIRACLES! NO MIRACLES TODAY! THEY'VE BEEN ALL USED UP! IT'S ONLY ME! MR. SLAVE LABOR HIMSELF COME HOME TO REPLENISH THE EMPTY LARDER!

WESLEY: What're you yelling for? There's nobody here.

WESTON *wheels around facing* WESLEY. WESLEY *stays still.*

WESTON: What the hell are you sneakin' up like that for? You coulda' got yourself killed!

WESLEY: What's in the bag?

WESTON: Groceries! What else. Somebody's gotta' feed this house.

WESTON *turns back to refrigerator and goes on putting more artichokes into it.*

WESLEY: What kind of groceries?

WESTON: Artichokes! What do you think?

WESLEY: *(coming closer)* Artichokes?

WESTON: Yeah. Good desert artichokes. Picked 'em up for half-price out in Hot Springs.

WESLEY: You went all the way out there for artichokes?

WESTON: 'Course not! What do you think I am, an idiot or something? I went out there to check on my land.

WESLEY: What land?

WESTON: My desert land! Now stop talking! Everything was all right until you came in. I was talking to myself and everything was all right.

WESTON *empties the bag into the refrigerator, then slams the door shut. He crunches up the bag and crosses back to the table. He opens up his bag of laundry and starts taking dirty clothes out and stacking them in piles on the table.* WESLEY *crosses to refrigerator and opens it, looks in at artichokes. He takes one out and looks at it closely, then puts it back in. They keep talking through all this.*

WESLEY: I didn't know you had land in the desert.

WESTON: 'Course I do. I got an acre and a half out there.

WESLEY: You never told me.

WESTON: Why should I tell you? I told your mother.

WESLEY: She never told me.

WESTON: Aw, shut up, will ya'?

WESLEY: What kind of land is it?

WESTON: It's not what I expected, that's for sure.

WESLEY: What is it, then?

WESTON: It's just not what I expected. Some guy came to the door selling land. So I bought some.

WESLEY: What guy?

WESTON: Some guy. Looked respectable. Talked a real good line. Said it was an investment for the future. All kinds of great things were going to be developed. Golf courses, shopping centers, banks, sauna baths. All that kinda' stuff. So I bought it.

WESLEY: How much did you pay?

WESTON: Well, I didn't pay the whole thing. I put something down on it. I'm not stupid.

WESLEY: How much?

WESTON: Why should I tell you? I borrowed it, so it's none of your goddamn business how much it was!

WESLEY: But it turned out to be a hoax, huh?

WESTON: A real piece of shit. Just a bunch of strings on sticks, with the lizards blowing across it.

WESLEY: Nothing around it?

WESTON: Not a thing. Just desert. No way to even get water to the goddamn place. No way to even set a trailer on it.

WESLEY: Where's the guy now?

WESTON: How should I know! Where's your mother anyway?

WESLEY: *(shutting refrigerator)* She went out.

WESTON: Yeah, I know she went out. The car's gone. Where'd she go to?

WESLEY: Don't know.

WESTON: *(bundling up empty duffel bag under his arm)* Well, when she gets back tell her to do this laundry for me. Tell her not to put bleach in anything but the socks and no starch in the collars. Can you remember that?

WESLEY: Yeah, I think so. No bleach and no starch.

WESTON: That's it. You got it. Now don't forget. *(he heads for stage right)*

WESLEY: Where are you going?

WESTON: Just never mind where I'm going! I can take care of myself. *(he stops and looks at the lamb)* What's the matter with the lamb?

WESLEY: Maggots.

WESTON: Poor little bugger. Put some a' that blue shit on it. That'll fix him up. You know that blue stuff in the bottle?

WESLEY: Yeah.

WESTON: Put some a' that on it. *(pauses a second, looks around)* You know I was even thinkin' a' sellin' this place.

WESLEY: You were?

WESTON: Yeah. Don't tell your mother though.

WESLEY: I won't.

WESTON: Bank probably won't let me, but I was thinkin' I could sell it and buy some land down in Mexico.

WESLEY: Why down there?

WESTON: I like it down there. *(looks at lamb again)* Don't forget about that blue stuff. Can't afford to lose any lambs. Only had but two sets a' twins this year, didn't we?

WESLEY: Three.

WESTON: Well, three then. It's not much.

WESTON *exits stage right.* WESLEY *looks at lamb. Lights fade to black.*

ACT 2

SCENE:

Same set. Loud hammering and sawing heard in darkness. Lights come up slowly on WESLEY *building a new door center stage. Hammers, nails, saw, and wood lying around, sawdust on floor. The fence enclosure and the lamb are gone. A big pot of artichokes is boiling away on the stove.* WESTON's *dirty laundry is still in piles on the table.* EMMA *sits at the stage left end of the table making a new set of charts for her demonstration with magic markers and big sheets of cardboard. She is dressed in jodhpurs, riding boots, and a western shirt. Lights up full. They each continue working at their*

separate tasks in silence, each of them totally concentrated. WES-
LEY *measures wood with a tape measure and then cuts it on one of
the chairs with the saw. He nails pieces together. After a while they
begin talking but still concentrate on their work.*

EMMA: Do you think she's making it with that guy?

WESLEY: Who, Taylor? How should I know?

EMMA: I think she is. She's after him for his money.

WESLEY: He's after our money. Why should she be after his?

EMMA: What money?

WESLEY: Our potential money.

EMMA: This place couldn't be that valuable.

WESLEY: Not the way it is now, but they'll divide it up. Make lots out
of it.

EMMA: She's after more than that.

WESLEY: More than what?

EMMA: Money. She's after esteem.

WESLEY: With Taylor?

EMMA: Yeah. She sees him as an easy ticket. She doesn't want to be
stuck out here in the boonies all her life.

WESLEY: She shoulda' thought of that a long time ago.

EMMA: She couldn't. Not with Pop. He wouldn't let her think. She just
went along with things.

WESLEY: She can't think. He can't either.

EMMA: Don't be too harsh.

WESLEY: How can they think when they're behind the eight ball all the
time. They don't have time to think.

EMMA: How come you didn't tell me when Pop came in last night?

WESLEY: I don't know.

EMMA: You could've told me.

WESLEY: He just brought his dirty laundry and then left.

EMMA: He brought food, too.

WESLEY: Artichokes.

EMMA: Better than nothing. *(pause, as they work)* They're probably half
way to Mexico by now.

WESLEY: Who?

EMMA: She's snuggling up to him and giggling and turning the dial on
the radio. He's feeling proud of himself. He's buying her hot dogs
and bragging about his business.

WESLEY: She'll be back.

EMMA: She's telling him all about us and about how Dad's crazy and trying to kill her all the time. She's happy to be on the road. To see new places go flashing by. They cross the border and gamble on the jai alai games. They head for Baja and swim along the beaches. They build campfires and roast fish at night. In the morning they take off again. But they break down somewhere outside a little place called Los Cerritos. They have to hike five miles into town. They come to a small beat-up gas station with one pump and a dog with three legs. There's only one mechanic in the whole town, and that's me. They don't recognize me though. They ask if I can fix their "carro," and I speak only Spanish. I've lost the knack for English by now. I understand them though and give them a lift back up the road in my rebuilt four-wheel-drive International. I jump out and look inside the hood. I see that it's only the rotor inside the distributor that's broken, but I tell them that it needs an entire new generator, a new coil, points and plugs, and some slight adjustments to the carburetor. It's an overnight job, and I'll have to charge them for labor. So I set a cot up for them in the garage, and after they've fallen asleep I take out the entire engine and put in a rebuilt Volkswagen block. In the morning I charge them double for labor, see them on their way, and then resell their engine for a small mint.

WESLEY: If you're not doing anything, would you check the artichokes?

EMMA: I am doing something.

WESLEY: What?

EMMA: I'm remaking my charts.

WESLEY: What do you spend your time on that stuff tor? You should be doing more important stuff.

EMMA: Like checking artichokes?

WESLEY: Yeah!

EMMA: You check the artichokes. I'm busy.

WESLEY: You're on the rag.

EMMA: Don't get personal. It's not nice. You should have more consideration.

WESLEY: Just put some water in them, would you? Before they burn.

EMMA *throws down her magic marker and crosses to the pot of artichokes. She looks in the pot and then crosses back to her chair and goes on working on her charts.*

WESLEY: Are they all right?

EMMA: Perfect. Just like a little boiling paradise in a pot. What're you making anyway?

WESLEY: A new door. What's it look like?

EMMA: Looks like a bunch of sawed-up wood to me.

WESLEY: At least it's practical.

EMMA: We're doing okay without a front door. Besides it might turn off potential buyers. Makes the place look like a chicken shack. *(remembers her chicken)* Oh, my chicken! ⟩ I could've killed her right then.

WESLEY: You don't understand what's happening yet, do you?

EMMA: With what?

WESLEY: The house. You think it's Mr. and Mrs. America who're gonna' buy this place, but it's not. It's Taylor.

EMMA: He's a lawyer.

WESLEY: He works for an agency. Land development.

EMMA: So what?

WESLEY: So it means more than losing a house. It means losing a country.

EMMA: You make it sound like an invasion.

WESLEY: It is. It's a zombie invasion. Taylor is the head zombie. He's the scout for the other zombies. He's only a sign that more zombies are on their way. They'll be filing through the door pretty soon.

EMMA: Once you get it built.

WESLEY: There'll be bulldozers crashing through the orchard. There'll be giant steel balls crashing through the walls. There'll be foremen with their sleeves rolled up and blueprints under their arms. There'll be steel girders spanning acres of land. Cement pilings. Prefab walls. Zombie architecture, owned by invisible zombies, built by zombies for the use and convenience of all other zombies. A zombie city! Right here! Right where we're living now.

EMMA: We could occupy it. Dad's got a gun.

WESLEY: It's a Jap gun.

EMMA: It works. I saw him shoot a peacock with it once.

WESLEY: A peacock?

EMMA: Blasted it to smithereens. It was sitting right out there in the sycamore tree. It was screaming all night long.

WESLEY: Probably mating season.

EMMA: *(after long pause)* You think they'll come back?

WESLEY: Who?

EMMA: Our parents.

WESLEY: You mean ever?

31

EMMA: Yeah. Maybe they'll never come back, and we'll have the whole place to ourselves. We could do a lot with this place.

WESLEY: I'm not staying here forever.

EMMA: Where are you going?

WESLEY: I don't know. Alaska, maybe.

EMMA: Alaska?

WESLEY: Sure. Why not?

EMMA: What's in Alaska?

WESLEY: The frontier.

EMMA: Are you crazy? It's all frozen and full of rapers.

WESLEY: It's full of possibilities. It's undiscovered.

EMMA: Who wants to discover a bunch of ice?

> WESTON *suddenly stumbles on from stage right. He's considerably drunker than the last time.* EMMA *stands at the table, not knowing whether to stay or leave.* WESTON *looks at her.*

WESTON: *(to EMMA)* Just relax. Relax! It's only your old man. Sit down!

> EMMA *sits again.* WESLEY *stands by awkwardly.* WESTON *looks at the wood on the floor.*

WESTON: *(to WESLEY)* What the hell's all this? You building a barn in here or something?

WESLEY: New door.

WESTON: What! Don't talk with your voice in the back of your throat like a worm! Talk with your teeth! Talk!

WESLEY: I am talking.

WESTON: All right. Now I asked you what all this is. What is all this?

WESLEY: It's a new door.

WESTON: What's a new door? What's the matter with the old door?

WESLEY: It's gone.

> WESTON *turns around, weaving slightly, and looks off stage right.*

WESTON: Oh. *(he turns back to* WESLEY*)* Where'd it go?

WESLEY: You broke it down.

WESTON: Oh. *(he looks toward table)* My laundry done yet?

EMMA: She didn't come back yet.

WESTON: Who didn't?

EMMA: Mom.

WESTON: She didn't come back yet? It's been all night. Hasn't it been all night?

EMMA: Yes.

WESTON: Hasn't the sun rised and falled on this miserable planet?

EMMA: Yes.

WESTON: *(turning to* WESLEY*)* So where's she been?

WESLEY: Don't know.

WESTON: Don't pull that one! Don't pull that one on me!

He starts to come after WESLEY. WESLEY *backs off fast.* WESTON *stops. He stands there weaving in place.*

WESLEY: I don't know. Really.

WESTON: Don't try protecting her! There's no protection! Understand! None! She's had it!

WESLEY: I don't know where she went.

EMMA: She went with a lawyer.

WESTON *turns to* EMMA *slowly.*

WESTON: A what?

EMMA: A lawyer.

WESTON: What's a lawyer? A law man? A person of the law? *(suddenly yelling)* WHAT'S A LAWYER?

EMMA: A guy named Taylor.

Long pause, as WESTON *stares at her drunkenly, trying to fathom it. Then he turns to* WESLEY.

WESTON: *(to* WESLEY*)* Taylor? You knew?

WESLEY: I thought she'd be back by now. She said she was going out for a business lunch.

WESTON: You knew!

EMMA: Maybe they had an accident.

WESTON: *(to* EMMA*)* In my car! In my Kaiser-Fraser! I'll break his fuck- ing back!

WESLEY: Maybe they did have an accident. I'll call the hospitals.

WESTON: DON'T CALL ANYBODY! *(quieter)* Don't call anybody. *(pause)* That car was an antique. Worth a fortune.

EMMA: *(after long pause)* You wanna' sit down, Pop?

WESTON: I'm standing. What's that smell in here? What's that smell!

WESLEY: Artichokes.

WESTON: They smell like that?

WESLEY: They're boiling.

WESTON: Stop them from boiling! They might boil over.

WESLEY *goes to stove and turns it off.*

WESTON: Where's that goddamn sheep you had in here? Is that what you're building? A barn for that sheep?

WESLEY: A door.

WESTON: *(staggering)* I gotta' sit down.

He stumbles toward table and sits at stage right end. EMMA *stands.*

WESTON: *(to* EMMA*)* Sit down! Sit back down! Turn off those artichokes!

WESLEY: I did.

WESTON: *(pushing laundry to one side)* She didn't do any of this. It's the same as when I brought it. None of it!

EMMA: I'll do it.

WESTON: No, you won't do it! You let her do it! It's her job! What does she do around here anyway? Do you know? What does she do all day long? What does a woman do?

EMMA: I don't know.

WESTON: You should be in school.

EMMA: It's all right if I do it. I don't mind doing it.

WESTON: YOU'RE NOT DOING IT! *(long silence)* What do you think of this place?

EMMA: The house?

WESTON: The whole thing. The whole fandango! The orchard! The air! The night sky!

EMMA: It's all right.

WESTON: *(to* WESLEY*)* What do you think of it?

WESLEY: I wouldn't sell it.

WESTON: You wouldn't sell it. You couldn't sell it! It's not yours!

WESLEY: I know. But I wouldn't if it was.

WESTON: How come? What good is it? What good's it doing?

WESLEY: It's just here. And we're on it. And we wouldn't be if it got sold.

WESTON: Very sound reasoning. Very sound. *(turns to* EMMA*)* Your brother never was much in the brain department, was he? You're the one who's such a smart-ass. You're the straight-A student, aren't you?

EMMA: Yes.

WESTON: Straight-A's and you're moldering around this dump. What're you going to do with yourself?

EMMA: I don't know.

WESTON: You don't know. Well you better think of something fast, because I've found a buyer. *(silence)* I've found someone to give me cash. Cash on the line! *(he slams table with his hand. Long silence, then* EMMA *gets up and exits off left)*

WESTON: What's the matter with her?

WESLEY: I don't know. She's got her first period.

WESTON: Her what? She's too young for that. That's not supposed to happen when they're that age. It's premature.

WESLEY: She's, got it.

WESTON: What happens when I'm gone, you all sit around and talk about your periods? You're not supposed to know when your sister has her period! That's confidential between women. They keep it a secret that means.

WESLEY: I know what "confidential" means.

WESTON: Good.

WESLEY: Why don't you go to bed or something, so I can finish this door.

WESTON: What for? I told ya' I'm selling the joint. Why build a new door? No point in putting money into it.

WESLEY: I'm still living here. I'm living here right up to the point when I leave.

WESTON: Very brave. Very courageous outlook. I envy it in fact.

WESLEY: You do?

WESTON: Sure! Of course! What else is there to envy but an outlook? Look at mine! Look at my outlook. You don't envy it, right?

WESLEY: No.

WESTON: That's because it's full of poison. Infected. And you recognize poison, right? You recognize it when you see it?

WESLEY: Yes.

WESTON: Yes, you do. I can see that you do. My poison scares you.

WESLEY: Doesn't scare me.

WESTON: No?

WESLEY: No.

WESTON: Good. You're growing up. I never saw my old man's poison until I was much older than you. Much older. And then you know how I recognized it?

WESLEY: How?

WESTON: Because I saw myself infected with it. That's how. I saw me carrying it around. His poison in my body. You think that's fair?

WESLEY: I don't know.

WESTON: Well, what do you think? You think I asked for it?

WESLEY: No.

WESTON: So it's unfair, right?

WESLEY: It's just the way it happened.

WESTON: I didn't ask for it, but I got it.

WESLEY: What is it anyway?

WESTON: What do you mean, what is it? You can see it for yourself!

WESLEY: I know it's there, but I don't know what it is.

WESTON: You'll find out.

WESLEY: How?

WESTON: How do you poison coyotes?

WESLEY: Strychnine.

WESTON: How! Not what!

WESLEY: You put it in the belly of a dead lamb.

WESTON: Right. Now do you see?

WESLEY: *(after pause)* No.

WESTON: You're thick! You're really thick. *(pause)* You know I watched my old man move around. I watched him move through rooms. I watched him drive tractors, watched him watching baseball, watched him keeping out of the way of things. Out of the way of my mother. Away from my brothers. Watched him on the sidelines. Nobody saw him but me. Everybody was right there, but nobody saw him but me. He lived apart. Right in the midst of things and he lived apart. Nobody saw that.

Long pause.

WESLEY: You want an artichoke?

WESTON: No.

WESLEY: Who's the buyer?

WESTON: Some guy. Owns the "Alibi Club" downtown. Said he'll give me cash.

WESLEY: How much?

WESTON: Enough to get to Mexico. They can't touch me down there.

WESLEY: Who?

WESTON: None of your goddamn business! Why is it you always drive yourself under my skin when I'm around? Why is that?

WESLEY: We don't get along.

WESTON: Very smart! Very observant! What's the matter with you anyway? What're you doing around here?

WESLEY: I'm part of your offspring.

WESTON: Jesus, you're enough to drive a sane man crazy! You're like having an espionage spy around. Why are you watching me all the time?

WESTON *looks at him. They stare at each other for a moment.*

WESTON: You can watch me all you want to. You won't find out a thing.

WESLEY: Mom's trying to sell the place, too.

WESTON *looks at him hard.*

WESLEY: That's who the lawyer guy was. She's selling it through him.

WESTON *stands and almost topples over.*

WESTON: I'LL KILL HER! I'LL KILL BOTH OF THEM! Where's my gun? I had a gun here! A captured gun!

WESLEY: Take it easy.

WESTON: No, you take it easy! This whole thing has gone far enough! It's like living in a den of vipers! Spies! Conspiracies behind my back! I'M BEING TAKEN FOR A RIDE BY EVERY ONE OF YOU! I'm the one who works! I'm the one who brings home food! THIS IS MY HOUSE! I BOUGHT THIS HOUSE! AND I'M SELLING THIS HOUSE! AND I'M TAKING ALL THE MONEY BECAUSE IT'S OWED ME! YOU ALL OWE IT TO ME! EVERY LAST ONE OF YOU! SHE CAN'T STEAL THIS HOUSE AWAY FROM ME! IT'S MINE!

He falls into table and collapses on it. He tries to keep himself from falling to the floor. WESLEY *moves toward him.*

WESTON: JUST KEEP BACK! I'M NOT DYING, SO JUST KEEP BACK!

He struggles to pull himself up on the table, knocking off dirty laundry and EMMA'*s charts.*

WESTON: I don't need a bed. I don't need anything from you! I'll stay right here. DON'T ANYONE TRY TO MOVE ME! NOBODY! I'm staying right here.

He finally gets on table so that he's lying flat out on it. He slowly goes unconscious. WESLEY *watches him from a safe distance.*

WESLEY: (*still standing there watching* WESTON) EMMA! (*no answer*) Oh, shit. Don't go out on me. Pop?

He moves toward WESTON *cautiously.* WESTON *comes to suddenly. Still lying on table.*

WESTON: DON'T GET TOO CLOSE!

WESLEY *jumps back.*

WESLEY: Wouldn't you rather be on the bed?

WESTON: I'm all right here. I'm numb. Don't feel a thing. Feels good to be numb.

WESLEY: We don't have to sell, you know. We could fix the place up.

WESTON: It's too late for that. I owe money.

WESLEY: I could get a job.

WESTON: You're gonna' have to.

WESLEY: I will. We could work this place by ourselves.

WESTON: Don't be stupid. There's not enough trees to make a living.

WESLEY: We could join that California Avocado Association. We could make a living that way.

WESTON: Get out of here! Get away from me!

WESLEY: Taylor can't buy this place without your signature.

WESTON: I'll kill him! If I have to, I'll kill myself along with him. I'll crash into him. I'll crash the Packard right into him. What's he look like? *(no answer from* WESLEY*)* WHAT'S HE LOOK LIKE?

WESLEY: Ordinary. Like a crook.

WESTON: *(still lying on table)* I'll find him. Then I'll find that punk who sold me that phony desert land. I'll track them all down. Every last one of them. Your mother too. I'll track her down and shoot them in their bed. In their hotel bed. I'll splatter their brains all over the vibrating bed. I'll drag him into the hotel lobby and slit his throat. I was in the war. I know how to kill. I was over there. I know how to do it. I've done it before. It's no big deal. You just make an adjustment. You convince yourself it's all right. That's all. It's easy. You just slaughter them. Easy.

WESLEY: You don't have to kill him. It's illegal, what he's doing.

WESTON: HE'S WITH MY WIFE! THAT'S ILLEGAL!

WESLEY: She'll come back.

WESTON: He doesn't know what he's dealing with. He thinks I'm just like him. Cowardly. Sniveling. Sneaking around. He's not counting on what's in my blood. He doesn't realize the explosiveness. We don't belong to the same class. He doesn't realize that. He's not counting on that. He's counting on me to use my reason. To talk things out. To have a conversation. To go out and have a business lunch and talk things over. He's not counting on murder. Murder's the farthest thing from his mind.

WESLEY: Just take it easy, Pop. Try to get some sleep.

38

WESTON: I am sleeping! I'm sleeping right here. I'm falling away. I was a flyer you know.

WESLEY: I know.

WESTON: I flew giant machines in the air. Giants! Bombers. What a sight. Over Italy. The Pacific. Islands. Giants. Oceans. Blue oceans.

Slowly WESTON *goes unconscious again as* WESLEY *watches him lying on table.* WESLEY *moves toward him slightly.*

WESLEY Pop? *(he moves in a little closer)* You asleep?

He turns downstage and looks at the wood and tools. He looks toward the refrigerator. ELLA *enters from down right carrying a bag of groceries. She stops when she sees* WESLEY. WESLEY *turns toward her.* ELLA *looks at* WESTON *lying on the table.*

ELLA: How long's he been here?

WESLEY: Just got here. Where have you been?

ELLA: *(crossing to refrigerator)* Out.

WESLEY: Where's your boyfriend?

ELLA: *(opening refrigerator)* Don't get insulting. Who put all these artichokes in here? What's going on?

WESLEY: Dad. He brought them back from the desert.

ELLA: What desert?

WESLEY: Hot Springs.

ELLA: Oh. He went down to look at his pathetic piece of property, I guess.

ELLA *sets the bag of groceries on the stove, then starts throwing the artichokes out onto the floor from the refrigerator.*

WESLEY: What are you doing?

ELLA: Throwing these out. It's a joke bringing artichokes back here when we're out of food.

WESLEY: How do you know about his desert property?

ELLA: I just know, that's all.

WESLEY: He told you? He never told me about it.

ELLA: I just happen to know he was screwed out of five hundred bucks. Let's leave it at that. Another shrewd business deal.

WESLEY: Taylor.

ELLA: *(turning to* WESLEY*)* What?

WESLEY: Taylor sold it to him right?

ELLA: Don't be ridiculous. *(turns back to refrigerator)*

WESLEY: How else would you know?

ELLA: He's not the only person in the world involved in real estate, you know.

WESLEY: He's been sneaking around here for months.

ELLA: Sneaking? He doesn't sneak. He comes right to the front door every time. He's very polite.

WESLEY: He's venomous.

ELLA: You're just jealous of him, that's all.

WESLEY: Don't give me that shit! It was him, wasn't it? I remember seeing him with his briefcase, wandering around the property.

ELLA: He's a speculator. That's his job. It's very important in this day and age to have someone who can accurately assess the value of land. To see its potential for the future.

She starts putting all the groceries from her bag into the re-frigerator.

WESLEY: What exactly is he anyway? You told me he was a lawyer.

ELLA: I don't delve into his private affairs.

WESLEY: You don't, huh?

ELLA: Why are you so bitter all of a sudden?

WESLEY: It's not all of a sudden.

ELLA: I should think you'd be very happy to leave this place. To travel. To see other parts of the world.

WESLEY: I'm not leaving!

ELLA: Oh, yes you are. We all are. I've sealed the deal. It just needs one last little signature from me and its finished. Everything. The beat-up cars, the rusted out tractor, the moldy avocados, the insane horse, the demented sheep, the chickens, the whole entire shooting match. The whole collection. Over.

WESLEY: Then you're free I suppose?

ELLA: Exactly.

WESLEY: Are you going off with him?

ELLA: I wish you'd get your mind out of the garbage. I'm on my own.

WESLEY: Where'd you get the groceries?

ELLA: I picked them up.

WESLEY: *(after pause)* You know, you're too late. All your wheeling and dealing and you've missed the boat.

ELLA: *(closing refrigerator, turning to* WESLEY*)* What do you mean?

WESLEY: Dad's already sold it.

ELLA: You must be crazy! He couldn't sell a shoestring! Look at him!

Look at him lying there! Does that look like a man who could sell something as valuable as a piece of property? Does that look like competence to you? Take a look at him! He's pathetic!

WESLEY: I wouldn't wake him up if I were you.

ELLA: He can't hurt me now! I've got protection! If he lays a hand on me, I'll have him cut to ribbons! He's finished!

WESLEY: He's beat you to the punch and he doesn't even know it.

ELLA: Don't talk stupid! And get this junk out of here! I'm tired of looking at broken doors every time I come in here.

WESLEY: That's a new door.

ELLA: GET IT OUT OF HERE!

WESLEY: *(quietly)* I told you, you better not wake him up.

ELLA: I'm not tiptoeing around anymore. I'm finished with feeling like a foreigner in my own house. I'm not afraid of him anymore.

WESLEY: You should be. He's going to kill Taylor, you know.

ELLA: He's always going to kill somebody! Every day he's going to kill somebody!

WESLEY: He means it this time. He's got nothing to lose.

ELLA: That's for sure!

WESLEY: He's going to kill you, too.

ELLA *is silent for a while. They look at each other.*

ELLA: Do you know what this is? It's a curse. I can feel it. It's invisible but it's there. It's always there. It comes onto us like nighttime. Every day I can feel it. Every day I can see it coming. And it always comes. Repeats itself. It comes even when you do everything to stop it from coming. Even when you try to change it. And it goes back. Deep. It goes back and back to tiny little cells and genes. To atoms. To tiny little swimming things making up their minds without us. Plotting in the womb. Before that even. In the air. We're surrounded with it. It's bigger than government even. It goes forward too. We spread it. We pass it on. We inherit it and pass it down, and then pass it down again. It goes on and on like that without us.

ELLIS, *the owner of the "Alibi Club," enters from right and smiles at them. He is wearing a shiny yellow shirt, open at the collar, with a gold cross on a chain hanging from his neck. He's very burly, with tattooes all over his arms, tight-fitting pants, shiny shoes, lots of rings. He looks around and notices* WESTON *still lying on the table.*

41

ELLIS: A few too many "boiler-makers," huh? I keep telling him to go light, but it's like fartin' in the wind. *(laughs at his own joke)* You must be the wife and kids. Name's Ellis, I run the "Alibi Club," down in town. You must know it, huh?
No reaction from ELLA and WESLEY.

ELLIS: Well, the old man knows it, that's for sure. Down there pretty near every night. Regular steady. Always wondered where he slept. What's that smell in here?

WESLEY: Artichokes.

ELLIS: Artichokes, huh? Smells like stale piss. *(bursts out laughing; no reaction from others)* Never was big on vegetables myself. I'm a steak man. "Meat and blood," that's my motto. Keeps your bones hard as ivory.

ELLA: I know it may be asking a little bit too much to knock when there's no door to knock on, but do you always make a habit of just wandering into people's houses like you own them?

ELLIS: I do own it. *(pause)* That's right. Signed, sealed, and delivered. Got the cash right here.
He pulls out two big stacks of bills from his belt and waves them in the air.

ELLIS: Fifteen hundred in hard core mean green.

WESLEY: Fifteen hundred dollars! *(looks at ELLA)*

ELLIS: That's what he owes. That's the price we agreed on. Look, buddy, I didn't even have to show up here with it. Your old man's such a sap he signed the whole thing over to me without a dime even crossing the bar. I coulda' stung him easy. Just happens that I'm a man of honor.

ELLA: *(to WESLEY)* Get him out of here!

ELLIS: *(coldly to WESLEY)* I wouldn't try it, buddy boy.
ELLIS and WESLEY stare at each other. ELLIS smiles.

ELLIS: I've broken too many backs in my time, buddy. I'm not a hard man, but I'm strong as a bull calf, and I don't realize my own strength. It's terrible when that happens. You know? Before you know it, someone's hurt. Someone's lying there.

ELLA: This is a joke! You can't buy a piece of property from an alcoholic! He's not responsible for his actions!

ELLIS: He owns it, doesn't he?

ELLA: I OWN IT!

ELLIS: That's not what he told me.

ELLA: I own it and it's already been sold, so just get the hell out!

ELLIS: Well, I've got the deed right here. *(he pulls deed out)* Right here. Signed, sealed, and delivered. How do you explain that?

ELLA: It's not legal!

WESLEY: Who does he owe money to?

ELLIS: Oh, well, now I don't stick my nose where it doesn't belong. I just happen to know that he owes to some pretty hard fellas.

WESLEY: Fifteen hundred bucks?

ELLIS: That's about the size of it.

ELLA: Wake him up! We'll get to the bottom of this.

WESLEY: *(to* ELLA*)* Are you crazy? If he sees you here he'll go off the deep end.

ELLA: *(going to* WESTON *and shaking him)* I'll wake him up, then!

WESLEY: Oh, Jesus!

WESTON *remains unconscious.* ELLA *keeps shaking him violently.*

ELLA: Weston! Weston get up! Weston!

ELLIS: I've seen some hard cases in my time, but he's dedicated. That's for sure. Drinks like a Canadian. Flat out.

WESLEY: You say these guys are tough? What does he owe them for?

ELLIS: Look, buddy, he borrows all the time. He's a borrowing fool. It could be anything. Payments on a car. Land in the desert. He's always got some fool scheme going. He's just let it slide too long this time, that's all.

WESLEY: What'll they do to him?

ELLIS: Nothing now. I've saved his hide. You should be kissing my feet.

ELLA: WESTON! GET UP!

She is tiring from shaking him. WESTON *remains unconscious.*

WESLEY: They'd kill him for fifteen hundred bucks?

ELLIS: Who said anything about killing? Did I say anything about killing?

WESLEY: No.

ELLIS: Then don't jump to conclusions. You can get in trouble that way.

WESLEY: Maybe you should deliver it to them.

ELLIS: Look, I've carried the ball this far, now he's gonna' have to do the rest. I'm not his bodyguard.

WESLEY: What if he takes off with it?

ELLIS: That's his problem.

43

WESLEY: Give it to me.

ELLIS: What?

WESLEY: The money. I'll deliver it.

ELLA: *(leaving* WESTON*)* Wesley, don't you touch that money! It's tainted! Don't you touch it!

ELLIS *and* WESLEY *look at each other.*

WESLEY: You've got the deed. I'm his oldest son.

ELLA: You're his only son!

WESLEY: Just give it to me. I'll take care of it.

ELLIS: *(handing money to* WESLEY*)* All right, buddy. Just don't go off half-cocked. That's a lot a' spendin' change for a young man.

WESLEY *takes it.*

ELLA: Wesley, it's illegal! You'll be an accomplice!

WESLEY: *(to* ELLIS*)* Where do I find them?

ELLIS: That's your business, buddy. I'm just the buyer.

ELLIS *walks around, looking over the place.* ELLA *crosses to* WESœ LEY *as* WESLEY *counts the money.*

ELLA: Wesley, you give me that money! It doesn't belong to you! Give it to me!

WESLEY: *(looking at her coldly)* There's not enough here to go to Europe on, Mom.

ELLIS: I was thinkin' of turning this place into a steak house. What do you think? Make a nice little steak house, don't you think?

WESLEY: *(still counting money)* Sure.

ELLIS: People stop in off the highway, have a steak, a martini, afternoon cocktail, look out over the valley. Nice and peaceful. Might even put in a Japanese garden out front. Have a few goldfish swimming around. Maybe an eight-hole pitch-and-putt course right out there, too. Place is full of potential.

ELLA: Wesley!

TAYLOR *appears with attaché case stage right.* ELLA *turns and sees him.* WESLEY *keeps counting money.*

TAYLOR: Oh. I'm sorry. I didn't realize you had company. *(to* ELLA*)* I've got the final draft drawn up.

TAYLOR *crosses toward table, sees* WESTON *lying on it, stops, looks for a place to set down his attaché case.*

ELLA: *(to* TAYLOR*)* It's too late.

TAYLOR: Excuse me? What's too late?

ELLA: The whole thing. Weston's sold it.

TAYLOR: That's silly. I've got the final draft right here in my case. All it needs is your signature.

ELLIS: Who's this character?

ELLA: *(to TAYLOR)* He sold it for fifteen hundred dollars.

TAYLOR: *(laughs)* That's impossible.

ELLA: There it is right there! Wesley's got it in his hands! Wesley's taking it!

TAYLOR: He can't sell this piece of property. He's incompetent. We've already been through that.

ELLIS: *(crossing to TAYLOR)* Hey, listen, buddy. I don't know what your story is, but I suggest you get the fuck outa' here because this is my deal here. Understand? This is my little package.

TAYLOR: *(to ELLA)* Who's this?

ELLA: He's the buyer.

WESLEY: *(to TAYLOR)* Too slow on the trigger, Taylor. Took it right out from under you, didn't he?

TAYLOR: Well, it's simply a matter of going to court then. He doesn't have a leg to stand on. Legally he's a ward of the state. He can't sell land.

ELLIS: *(waving deed)* Look, I checked this deed out at city hall, and everything's above board.

TAYLOR: The deed has nothing to do with it. I'm speaking of psychological responsibility.

WESLEY: Does that apply to buying the same as selling?

TAYLOR: *(to EMMA)* What's he talking about?

ELLA: Nothing. Wesley, you give that money back!

WESLEY: Does that apply to buying dried up land in the middle of the desert with no water and a hundred miles from the nearest gas pump?

TAYLOR: *(to WESLEY)* I think you're trying to divert the focus of the situation here. The point is that your father's psychologically and emotionally unfit to be responsible for his own actions, and, therefore, any legal negotiations issuing from him cannot be held binding. This can be easily proven in a court of law. We have first-hand evidence that he's prone to fits of violence. His license for driving has been revoked, and yet he still keeps driving. He's unable to get insurance. He's unable to hold a steady job. He's absent from his home ninety percent of the time. He has a jail record. It's an open and shut case.

ELLIS: *(to TAYLOR)* What are you anyway? A lawyer or something?

Where do you get off talkin' like that in my house!

ELLA: IT'S NOT YOUR HOUSE! THAT'S WHAT HE'S SAYING! CAN'T YOU LISTEN? DON'T YOU HAVE A BRAIN IN YOUR HEAD?

ELLIS: Listen, lady, I sell booze. You know what I mean? A lot a' weird stuff goes on in my bar, but I never seen anything as weird as this character. I never seen anything I couldn't handle.

WESLEY: You best take off, Taylor, before it all catches up to you.

TAYLOR: I refuse to be intimidated any further! I put myself out on a limb for this project and all I'm met with is resistance!

ELLA: I'm not resisting.

TAYLOR: *(to* WESLEY*)* You may not realize it, but there's corporations behind me! Executive management! People of influence. People with ambition who realize the importance of investing in the future. Of building this country up, not tearing it down. You people carry on as though the whole world revolved around your petty little existence. As though everything was holding its breath, waiting for your next move. Well, it's not like that! Nobody's waiting! Everything's going forward! Everything's going ahead without you! The wheels are in motion. There's nothing you can do to turn it back. The only thing you can do is cooperate. To play ball. To become part of us. To invest in the future of this great land. Because if you don't, you'll all be left behind. Every last one of you. Left high and dry. And there'll be nothing to save you. Nothing and nobody.

A policeman appears stage right in highway patrol gear.

SERGEANT MALCOLM: Uh—excuse me. Mrs. Tate?

ELLA: Yes.

MALCOLM: Are you Mrs. Tate?

ELLA: Yes, I am.

MALCOLM: I'm sorry. I would have knocked but there's no door.

ELLA: That's all right.

TAYLOR *begins to move to stage left nervously.* WESLEY *watches him.*

MALCOLM: I'm Sergeant Malcolm, Highway Patrol.

ELLA: Well, what is it?

MALCOLM: You have a daughter, Emma Tate?

ELLA: Yes. What's wrong?

MALCOLM: She's been apprehended.

ELLA: What for?

MALCOLM: It seems she rode her horse through a bar downtown and shot the place full of holes with a rifle.

ELLA: What?

ELLIS: What bar?

MALCOLM: Place called the "Alibi Club." I wasn't there at the time, but they picked her up.

ELLIS: That's my club!

MALCOLM: *(to* ELLIS*)* Are you the owner?

ELLIS: THAT'S MY CLUB!

MALCOLM: Are you Mr. Ellis?

ELLIS: What kind of damages?

MALCOLM: Well, we'll have to get an estimate, but it's pretty severe. Shot the whole place up. Just lucky there was no one in it at the time.

ELLIS: *(to* WESLEY*)* Give me that money back!

ELLIS *grabs money out of* WESLEY*'s hands.* TAYLOR *sneaks off stage left.*

WESLEY: *(to cop)* Hey! He's getting away! That guy's a crook!

MALCOLM: What guy?

WESLEY: *(moving toward stage left)* That guy! That guy who just ran out of here! He's an embezzler! A confidence man! Whatever you call it. He sold my old man phony land!

MALCOLM: That's not within my jurisdiction.

ELLIS: *(to* ELLA*)* I know he sent her down there. I wasn't born yesterday, ya' know! He's crazy if he thinks he can put that kind of muscle on me! What does he think he is anyway? I'm gonna' sue him blind for this! I'm gonna' take the shirt right off his back! I was trying to do him a favor! I was stickin' my neck out for him! You just tell him when he wakes up out of his stupor that he's in bigger trouble than he thinks! He ain't seen nothin' yet! You tell him. *(starts to leave)* And just remember that I own this place. It's mine! So don't try any more funny stuff. I got friends in high places, too. I deal directly with them all the time. Ain't that right, Sarge?

MALCOLM: I don't know about that. I'm here on other business.

ELLIS: *(to* ELLA*)* You just tell him! I'll teach him to mess around with me!

ELLIS *exits. Right.*

ELLA: *(to cop)* He's taking our money!

MALCOLM: Look, lady, your daughter's in jail. I don't know about any

47

of this other stuff. I'm here about your daughter.

WESLEY *runs off right.* ELLA *yells after him.*

ELLA: WESLEY! WHERE ARE YOU GOING?

WESLEY'S VOICE: *(off)* I'M GONNA' GET THAT MONEY BACK!

ELLA: IT'S NOT YOUR MONEY! COME BACK HERE! WESLEY! *(she stops and looks at* MALCOLM*)* Everybody's running off. Even Mr. Taylor. Did you hear the way he was talking to me? He was talking to me all different. All different than before. He wasn't nice at all.

MALCOLM: Mrs. Tate, what are we going to do about your daughter?

ELLA: I don't know. What should we do?

MALCOLM: Well, she has to stay in overnight, and if you don't want her back home she can be arraigned in juvenile court.

ELLA: We're all leaving here though. Everyone has to leave. She can't come home. There wouldn't be anyone here.

MALCOLM: You'll have to sign a statement then.

ELLA: What statement?

MALCOLM: Giving permission for the arraignment.

ELLA: All right.

MALCOLM: You'll have to come down with me unless you have a car.

ELLA: I have a car. *(pause)* Everyone's run away.

MALCOLM: Will you be all right by yourself?

ELLA: I am by myself.

MALCOLM: Yes, I know. Will you be all right or do you want to come with me in the patrol car?

ELLA: I'll be all right.

MALCOLM: I'll wait for you down at the station then.

MALCOLM *exits.* ELLA *just stands there.*

ELLA: *(to herself)* Everybody ran away.

WESTON *sits up with a jolt on the table.* ELLA *jumps. They look at each other for a moment, then* ELLA *runs off stage.* WESTON *just stays sitting up on the table. He looks around the stage. He gets to his feet and tries to steady himself. He walks toward the refrigerator and kicks the artichokes out of his way. He opens refrigerator and locks in. Lights slowly fade to black with* WESTON *standing there looking into refrigerator.*

ACT 3

SCENE:

Same set. Stage is cleared of wood and tools and artichokes. Fence enclosure with the lamb inside is back, center stage. Pot of fresh coffee heating on the stove. All the laundry has been washed and WESTON *is at the table to stage left folding it and stacking it in neat piles. He's minus his overcoat, baseball cap, and tennis shoes and wears a fresh clean shirt, new pants, shined shoes, and has had a shave. He seems sober now and in high spirits compared to before. The lamb is heard "baaing" in the dark as the lights slowly come up on* WESTON *at the table.*

WESTON: *(to lamb as he folds clothes)* There's worse things than maggots ya' know. Much worse. Maggots go away if they're properly attended to. If you got someone around who can take the time. Who can recognize the signs. Who brings ya' in out of the cold, wet pasture and sets ya' up in a cushy situation like this. No lamb ever had it better. It's warm. It's free of draft, now that I got the new door up. There's no varmints. No coyotes. No eagles. No— *(looks over at lamb)* Should I tell ya' something about eagles? This is a true story. This is a true account. One time I was out in the fields doing the castrating, which is a thing that has to be done. It's not my favorite job, but it's something that just has to be done. I'd set myself up right beside the lean-to out there. Just a little roof-shelter thing out there with my best knife, some boiling water, and a hot iron to cauterize with. It's a bloody job on all accounts. Well, I had maybe a dozen spring ram lambs to do out there. I had 'em all gathered up away from the ewes in much the same kinda' set up as you got right there. Similar fence structure like that. It was a crisp, bright type a' morning. Air was real thin and you could see all the way out across the pasture land. Frost was still well bit down on the stems, right close to the ground. Maybe a couple a' crows and the ewes carrying on about their babies, and that was the only sound. Well, I was working away out there when I feel this shadow cross over me. I could feel it even before I saw it take shape on the ground. Felt like the way it does when the clouds move across the sun. Huge and black and cold like. So I look up, half expecting a buzzard or maybe a red-tail, but what hits me across the eyes is this giant eagle. Now I'm a flyer and I'm used to aeronautics, but this sucker was doin' some downright suicidal antics. Real low down like he's coming in for a landing or something,

49

then changing his mind and pulling straight up again and sailing out away from me. So I watch him going small for a while, then turn back to my work. I do a couple more lambs maybe, and the same thing happens. Except this time he's even lower yet. Like I could almost feel his feathers on my back. I could hear his sound real clear. A giant bird. His wings made a kind of cracking noise. Then up he went again. I watched him longer this time, trying to figure out his intentions. Then I put the whole thing together. He was after those testes. Those fresh little remnants of manlihood. So I decided to oblige him this time and threw a few a' them on top a' the shed roof. Then I just went back to work again, pretending to be preoccupied. I was waitin' for him this time though. I was listening hard for him, knowing he'd be comin̥ in from behind me. I was watchin' the ground for any sign of blackness. Nothing happened for about three more lambs, when all of a sudden he comes. Just like a thunder clap. Blam! He's down on that shed roof with his talons taking half the tar paper with him, wings whippin' the air, screaming like a bred mare then climbing straight back up into the sky again. I had to stand up on that one. Somethin' brought me straight up off the ground and I started yellin' my head off. I don't know why it was comin' outa' me but I was standing there with this icy feeling up my backbone and just yelling my fool head off. Cheerin' for that eagle. I'd never felt like that since the first day I went up in a B-49. After a while I sat down again and went on workin'. And every time I cut a lamb I'd throw those balls up on top a' the shed roof. And every time he'd come down like the Cannonball Express on that roof. And every time I got that feeling.

WESLEY *appears stage right with his face and hands bloody.*

WESLEY: Then what?

WESTON: Were you listening to me?

WESLEY: What happens next?

WESTON: I was tellin' it to the lamb!

WESLEY: Tell it to me.

WESTON: You've already heard it. What happened to your face anyway?

WESLEY: Ran into a brick wall.

WESTON: Why don't ya' go clean up.

WESLEY: What happens next?

WESTON: I ain't tellin' it again!

WESLEY: Then I ain't cleaning up!

WESTON: What's the matter with you anyway? Are you drunk or something?

WESLEY: I was trying to get your money back.

WESTON: What money?

WESLEY: From Ellis.

WESTON: That punk. Don't waste your time. He's a punk crook.

WESLEY: He ran off with your money. And he's got the house too.

WESTON: I've got the house! I've decided to stay.

WESLEY: What?

WESTON: I'm stayin'. I finished the new door. Did you notice?

WESLEY: No.

WESTON: Well, you shoulda' noticed. You walked right through it. What's the matter with you? I'm fixin' the whole place up. I decided.

WESLEY: You're fixing it up?

WESTON: Yeah. That's what I said. What's so unusual about that? This could be a great place if somebody'd take some interest in it. Why don't you have some coffee and clean yourself up a little. You look like forty miles a' rough road. Go ahead. There's fresh coffee on the stove.

WESLEY *crosses slowly to the stove and looks at the coffee.*

WESTON: I got up and took a walk around the place. Bright and early. Don't think I've walked around the whole place for a couple a' years. I walked around and a funny thing started happening to me.

WESLEY: *(looking at coffee)* What?

WESTON: I started wondering who this was walking around in the orchard at six-thirty in the morning. It didn't feel like me. It was some character in a dark overcoat and tennis shoes and a baseball cap and stickers comin' out of his face. It didn't feel like the owner of a piece a' property as nice as this. Then I started to wonder who the owner was. I mean if I didn't feel like the owner, then who was the owner? I started wondering if the real owner was gonna' pop up out of nowhere and blast my brains out for trespassing. I started feeling like I should be running or hiding or something. Like I shouldn't be there in this kind of a neighborhood. Not that it's fancy or anything, but it's peaceful. It's real peaceful up here. Especially at that time a' the morning. Then it struck me that I actually was the owner. That somehow it was me and I was actually the one walking on my own piece of land. And that gave me a great feeling.

WESLEY: *(staring at coffee)* It did?

51

WESTON: Yeah. So I came back in here, and the first thing I did was I took all my old clothes off and walked around here naked. Just walked through the whole damn house in my birthday suit. Tried to get the feeling of it really being me in my own house. It was like peeling off a whole person. A whole stranger. Then I walked straight in and made myself a hot bath. Hot as I could stand it. Just sank down into it and let it sink deep into the skin. Let it fog up all the windows and the glass on the medicine cabinet. Then I let all the water drain out, and then I filled the whole tub up again but this time with ice cold water. Just sat there and let it creep up on me until I was in up to my neck. Then I got out and took a shave and found myself some clean clothes. Then I came in here and fixed myself a big old breakfast of ham and eggs.

WESLEY: Ham and eggs?

WESTON: Yeah. Somebody left a whole mess a' groceries in the ice box. Surprised the hell outa' me. Just like Christmas. Just like somebody knew I was gonna' be reborn this morning or something. Couldn't believe my eyes.

WESLEY *goes to refrigerator and looks in.*

WESTON: Then I started makin' coffee and found myself doing all this stuff I used to do. Like I was coming back to my life after a long time a' being away.

WESLEY: *(staring in refrigerator)* Mom brought this stuff.

WESTON: Then I started doing the laundry. All the laundry. I went around the house and found all the piles of dirty clothes I could get my hands on. Emma's, Ella's, even some a' yours. Some a' your socks. Found everybody's clothes. And every time I bent down to pick up somebody's clothes I could feel that person like they were right there in the room. Like the clothes were still attached to the person they belonged to. And I felt like I knew every single one of you. Every one. Like I knew you through the flesh and blood. Like our bodies were connected and we could never escape that. But I didn't feel like escaping. I felt like it was a good thing. It was good to be connected by blood like that. That a family wasn't just a social thing. It was an animal thing. It was a reason of nature that we were all together under the same roof. Not that we had to be but that we were supposed to be. And I started feeling glad about it. I started feeling full of hope.

WESLEY: *(staring in refrigerator)* I'm starving.

WESTON: *(crossing to WESLEY)* Look, go take a bath and get that crap off your face, and I'll make ya' some ham and eggs. What is that crap anyway?

WESLEY: Blood.

WESTON: He took a few swipes at ya', huh? Well go wash it off and come back in here. Go on!

WESLEY: *(turning to* WESTON*)* He wouldn't give me the money, you know.

WESTON: So what. The guy's a knuckle-head. Don't have the brains God gave a chicken. Now go in there and clean up before *I* start swingin' on you.

WESLEY exits off left. WESTON *starts taking ham and eggs out of refrigerator and fixing a breakfast at the stove. He yells off stage to* WESLEY *as he cooks.*

WESTON: *(yelling)* So I was thinkin' about that avocado deal you were talkin' about before! You know, joining up with the "Growers Association" and everything! And I was thinkin' it might not be such a bad deal after all! I mean we don't have to hire Chicanos or nothin'! We could pick 'em ourselves and sell 'em direct to the company! How 'bout that idea! Cut down on the overhead! That tractor's still workin', isn't it? I mean the motor's not seized up or nothin', and we got plenty a' good pressure in the irrigation! I checked it this morning! Water's blastin' right through those pipes! Wouldn't take much to get the whole operation goin' full-tilt again! I'll resell that piece a' land out there! That'll give us somethin' to get us started! Somebody somewhere's gonna' want a good piece a' desert land! It's prime location even if it isn't being developed! Only a three-hour drive from Palm Springs, and you know what that's like! You know the kinda' people who frequent that place! One of 'em's bound to have some extra cash!

ELLA enters from stage right. She looks haggard and tired. She stands there looking at WESTON, *who keeps cooking the eggs. Then she looks at the lamb.* WESTON *knows she's there but doesn't look at her.*

ELLA: *(after pause)* What's that lamb doing back in here?

WESTON: I got him back on his feet. It was nip and tuck there for a while. Didn't think he'd pull through. Maggots clear up into the small intestine.

ELLA: *(crossing to table)* Spare me the details.

She pulls off her white gloves and sits exhausted into the chair at stage right. She looks at the piles of clean laundry.

WESTON: *(still cooking)* Where you been anyway?

ELLA: Jail.

WESTON: Oh, they finally caught ya', huh? *(chuckles)*

ELLA: Very humorous.

WESTON: You want some breakfast? I was just fixin' something up for Wes, here.

ELLA: You're cooking?

WESTON: Yeah. What's it look like?

ELLA: Who did all this laundry?

WESTON: Yours truly.

ELLA: Are you having a nervous breakdown or what?

WESTON: Can't a man do his own laundry?

ELLA: As far as I know he can.

WESTON: Even did some a' yours too.

ELLA: Gee, thanks.

WESTON: Well, I coulda' just left it. I was doin' a load of my own, so I thought I'd throw everybody else's in to boot.

ELLA: I'm very grateful.

WESTON: So where you been? Off with that fancy lawyer?

ELLA: I've been to jail, like I said.

WESTON: Come on. What, on a visit? They throw you in the drunk tank? Out with it.

ELLA: I was visiting your daughter.

WESTON: Oh, yeah? What'd they nab her for?

ELLA: Possession of firearms. Malicious vandalism. Breaking and entering. Assault. Violation of equestrian regulations. You name it.

WESTON: Well, she always was a fireball.

ELLA: Part of the inheritance, right?

WESTON: Right. Direct descendant.

ELLA: Well, I'm glad you've found a way of turning shame into a source of pride.

WESTON: What's shameful about it? Takes courage to get charged with all that stuff. It's not everyone her age who can run up a list of credits like that.

ELLA: That's for sure.

WESTON: Could you?

ELLA: Don't be ridiculous! I'm not self-destructive. Doesn't run in my family line.

WESTON: That's right. I never thought about it like that. You're the only one who doesn't have it. Only us.

ELLA: Oh, so now I'm the outsider.

54

WESTON: Well, it's true. You come from a different class of people. Gentle. Artists. They were all artists, weren't they?

ELLA: My grandfather was a pharmacist.

WESTON: Well, scientists then. Members of the professions. Professionals. Nobody raised their voice.

ELLA: That's bad?

WESTON: No. Just different. That's all. Just different.

ELLA: Are we waxing philosophical over our eggs now? Is that the idea? Sobered up over night, have we? Awoken to a brand-new morning? What is this crap! I've been down there all night trying to pull Emma back together again and I come back to Mr. Hyde! Mr. "Goody Two-Shoes!" Mister Mia Copa himself! Well, you can kiss off with that crap because I'm not buying it!

WESTON: Would you like some coffee?

ELLA: NO, I DON'T WANT ANY GODDAMN COFFEE! AND GET THAT SON-OF-A-BITCHING SHEEP OUT OF MY KITCHEN!!

WESTON: *(staying cool)* You've picked up on the language okay, but your inflection's off.

ELLA: There's nothing wrong with my inflection!

WESTON: Something doesn't ring true about it. Something deep in the voice. At the heart of things.

ELLA: Oh, you are really something. How can you accuse me of not measuring up to your standards! You're a complete washout!

WESTON: It's got nothing to do with standards. It's more like fate.

ELLA: Oh, knock it off, would you? I'm exhausted.

WESTON: Try the table. Nice and hard. It'll do wonders for you.

ELLA: *(suddenly soft)* The table?

WESTON: Yeah. Just stretch yourself out. You'll be amazed. Better than any bed.

ELLA *looks at the table for a second, then starts pushing all the clean laundry off it onto the floor. She pulls herself up onto it and stretches out on it.* WESTON *goes on cooking with his back to her. She watches him as she lies there.*

WESTON: And when you wake up I'll have a great big breakfast of ham and eggs, ready and waiting. You'll feel like a million bucks. You'll wonder why you spent all those years in bed, once you feel that table. That table will deliver you.

WESLEY *wanders on stage from stage left, completely naked, his hair wet. He looks dazed.* WESTON *pays no attention but goes on*

55

preparing the breakfast and talking as WESLEY *wanders upstage and stares at* ELLA. *She looks at him but doesn't react. He turns downstage and looks at* WESTON. *He looks at lamb and crosses down to it. He bends over and picks it up, then carries it off stage right.* WESTON *goes on cooking and talking.* ELLA *stays on table.*

WESTON: That's the trouble with too much comfort, you know? Makes you forget where you come from. Makes you lose touch. You think you're making headway but you're losing all the time. You're falling behind more and more. You're going into a trance that you'll never come back from. You're being hypnotized. Your body's being mesmerized. You go into a coma. That's why you need a hard table once in a while to bring you back. A good hard table to bring you back to life.

ELLA: *(still on table, sleepily)* You should have been a preacher.

WESTON: You think so?

ELLA: Great voice you have. Deep. Resonates.

WESTON: *(putting eggs on plate)* I'm not a public person.

ELLA: I'm so exhausted.

WESTON: You just sleep.

ELLA: You should have seen that jail, Weston.

WESTON: I have.

ELLA: Oh, that's right. How could you ever sleep in a place like that?

WESTON: If you're numb enough you don't feel a thing. *(he yells off stage to* WESLEY*)* WES! YOUR BREAKFAST'S READY!

ELLA: He just went out.

WESTON: What?

ELLA: He just walked out stark naked with that sheep under his arm.

WESTON *looks at fence enclosure, sees lamb gone. He's still holding plate.*

WESTON: Where'd he go?

ELLA: Outside.

WESTON: *(crossing right, carrying plate)* WES! GODDAMNIT, YOUR BREAKFAST'S READY!

WESTON *exits carrying plate off stage right.* ELLA *tries to keep her eyes open, still on table.*

ELLA: *(to herself)* Nothing surprises me any more.

She slowly falls asleep on table. Nothing happens for a while. Then WESTON *comes back on from right still carrying plate.* ELLA *stays asleep on table.*

WESTON: *(crossing to stove)* He's not out there. Wouldn't ya' know it? Just when it's ready, he walks out. *(turning to ELLA)* Why'd he take the lamb? That lamb needs to be kept warm. *(sees that ELLA's sound asleep)* Great. *(turns and sets plate down on stove; looks at food)* Might as well eat it myself. A double breakfast. Why not? *(he starts eating off the plate, talks to himself)* Can't expect the thing to get well if it's not kept warm. *(he turns upstage again and looks at ELLA sleeping, then turns back to the plate of food)* Always was best at talkin' to myself. Always was the best thing. Nothing like it. Keeps ya' company at least.

WESLEY *enters from right dressed in* WESTON's *baseball cap, overcoat, and tennis shoes. He stands there.* WESTON *looks at him.* ELLA *sleeps.*

WESTON: What in the hell's goin' on with you? I was yellin' for you just now. Didn't you hear me?

WESLEY: *(staring at WESTON)* No.

WESTON: Your breakfast was all ready. Now it's cold. I've eaten half of it already. Almost half gone.

WESLEY: *(blankly)* You can have it.

WESTON: What're you doin' in those clothes anyway?

WESLEY: I found them.

WESTON: I threw them out! What's got into you? You go take a bath and then put on some old bum's clothes that've been thrown-up in, pissed in, and God knows what all in?

WESLEY: They fit me.

WESTON: I can't fathom you, that's for sure. What'd you do with that lamb?

WESLEY: Butchered it.

WESTON: *(turning away from him, disgusted)* I swear to God. *(pause, then turning to WESLEY)* WHAT'D YA' BUTCHER THE DUMB THING FOR!

WESLEY: We need some food.

WESTON: THE ICE BOX IS CRAMMED FULL A' FOOD!

WESLEY *crosses quickly to refrigerator, opens it, and starts pulling all kinds of food out and eating it ravenously.* WESTON *watches him, a little afraid of* WESLEY's *state.*

WESTON: WHAT'D YA' GO AND BUTCHER IT FOR? HE WAS GETTING BETTER! *(watches WESLEY eating hungrily)* What's a' matter with you, boy? I made ya' a big breakfast. Why didn't ya' eat that? What's the matter with you?

WESTON *moves cautiously, away from* WESLEY *to stage right.* WES-
LEY *keeps eating, throwing half-eaten food to one side and then
digging into more. He groans slightly as he eats.*

WESTON: *(to* WESLEY*)* Look, I know I ignored some a' the chores
around the place and you had to do it instead a' me. But I brought
you some artichokes back, didn't I? Didn't I do that? I didn't have
to do that. I went outa' my way. I saw the sign on the highway and
drove two miles outa' my way just to bring you back some artichokes. *(pause, as he looks at* WESLEY *eating; he glances nervously up at* ELLA, *then back to* WESLEY*)* You couldn't be all that
starving! We're not that bad off, goddamnit! I've seen starving
people in my time, and we're not that bad off! *(pause, no reaction
from* WESLEY, *who continues to eat ravenously)* You just been
spoiled, that's all! This is a paradise for a young person! There's
kids your age who'd give their eyeteeth to have an environment like
this to grow up in! You've got everything! Everything! Opportunity
is glaring you in the teeth here! *(turns toward* ELLA*)* ELLA! ELLA,
WAKE UP! *(no reaction from* ELLA; *turns back to* WESLEY, *still
eating)* If this is supposed to make me feel guilty, it's not working!
It's not working because I don't have to pay for my past now! Not
now! Not after this morning! All that's behind me now! YOU UN-
DERSTAND ME? IT'S ALL OVER WITH BECAUSE I'VE
BEEN REBORN! I'M A WHOLE NEW PERSON NOW! I'm a
whole new person.

WESLEY *stops eating suddenly and turns to* WESTON.

WESLEY: *(coldly)* They're going to kill you.

WESTON: *(pauses)* Who's going to kill me! What're you talking about!
Nobody's going to kill me!

WESLEY: I couldn't get the money.

WESTON: What money?

WESLEY: Ellis.

WESTON: So what?

WESLEY: You owe it to them.

WESTON: Owe it to who? I don't remember anything. All that's over
with now.

WESLEY: No, it's not. It's still there. Maybe you've changed, but you
still owe them.

WESTON: I can't remember. Must've borrowed some for the car pay-
ment. Can't remember it.

WESLEY: They remember it.

WESTON: So, I'll get it to them. It's not that drastic.

WESLEY: How? Ellis has the house and everything now.

WESTON: How does he have the house? This is my house!

WESLEY: You signed it over.

WESTON: I never signed anything!

WESLEY: You were drunk.

WESTON: SHUT UP!

WESLEY: How're you going to pay them?

WESTON: *(pause)* I can sell that land.

WESLEY: It's phony land. The guy's run off to Mexico.

WESTON: What guy?

WESLEY: Taylor. The lawyer. The lawyer friend of Mom's.

WESTON: *(pause, looks at* ELLA *sleeping, then back to* WESLEY*)* Same guy?

WESLEY: Same guy. Ripped us all off.

WESTON: This isn't right. I was on a whole new track. I was getting right up on top of it all.

WESLEY: They've got it worked out so you can't.

WESTON: I was ready for a whole new attack. This isn't right!

WESLEY: They've moved in on us like a creeping disease. We didn't even notice.

WESTON: I just built a whole new door and everything. I washed all the laundry. I cleaned up all the artichokes. I started over.

WESLEY: You better run.

WESTON: Run? What do you mean, run? I can't run!

WESLEY: Take the Packard and get out of here.

WESTON: I can't run out on everything.

WESLEY: Why not?

WESTON: 'CAUSE THIS IS WHERE I SETTLED DOWN! THIS IS WHERE THE LINE ENDED! RIGHT HERE! I MIGRATED TO THIS SPOT! I GOT NOWHERE TO GO TO! THIS IS IT!

WESLEY: Take the Packard.

WESTON *stands there for a while. He looks around, trying to figure a way out.*

WESTON: *(after pause)* I remember now. I was in hock. I was in hock up to my elbows. See, I always figured on the future. I banked on it. I was banking on it getting better. It couldn't get worse, so I figured it'd just get better. I figured that's why everyone wants you to buy things. Buy refrigerators. Buy cars, houses, lots, invest. They wouldn't be so generous if they didn't figure you had it

59

comin' in. At some point it had to be comin' in. So I went along with it. Why not borrow if you know it's coming in. Why not make a touch here and there. They all want you to borrow anyhow. Banks, car lots, investors. The whole thing's geared to invisible money. You never hear the sound of change any more. It's all plastic shuffling back and forth. It's all in everybody's heads. So I figured if that's the case, why not take advantage of it? Why not go in debt for a few grand if all it is is numbers? If it's all an idea and nothing's really there, why not take advantage? So I just went along with it, that's all. I just played ball.

WESLEY: You better go.

Pause, as WESTON *looks at* ELLA *sleeping.*

WESTON: Same guy, huh? She musta' known about it, too. She musta' thought I left her.

WESTON *turns and looks at* WESLEY. *Silence.*

WESLEY: You did.

WESTON: I just went off for a little while. Now and then. I couldn't stand it here. I couldn't stand the idea that everything would stay the same. That every morning it would be the same. I kept looking for it out there somewhere. I kept trying to piece it together. The jumps. I couldn't figure out the jumps. From being born, to growing up, to droppin' bombs, to having kids, to hittin' bars, to this. It all turned on me somehow. It all turned around on me. I kept looking for it out there somewhere. And all the time it was right inside this house.

WESLEY: They'll be coming for you here. They know where you live now.

WESTON: Where should I go?

WESLEY: How 'bout Mexico?

WESTON: Mexico? Yeah. That's where everyone escapes to, right? It's full of escape artists down there. I could go down there and get lost. I could disappear. I could start a whole new life down there.

WESLEY: Maybe.

WESTON: I could find that guy and get my money back. That real estate guy. What's his name?

WESLEY: Taylor.

WESTON: Yeah, Taylor. He's down there too, right? I could find him.

WESLEY: Maybe.

WESTON: *(looking over at* ELLA *again)* I can't believe she knew and still went off with him. She musta' thought I was dead or something. She musta' thought I was never coming back.

WESTON *moves toward* ELLA, *then stops. He looks at* WESLEY, *then turns and exits off right.* WESLEY *just stands there.* WESLEY *bends down and picks some scraps of food up off the floor and eats them very slowly. He looks at the empty lamb pen.* EMMA *enters from left, dressed as she was in Act 2. She crosses into center, looking in the direction of where* WESTON *went.* WESLEY *seems dazed as he slowly chews the food.* ELLA *stays asleep on table.* EMMA *carries a riding crop. She taps her leg with it as she looks off right.*

EMMA: Mexico, huh? He won't last a day down there. They'll find him easy. Stupid going to Mexico. That's the first place they'll look. *(to* WESLEY) What're you eating?

WESLEY: Food.

EMMA: Off the floor? You'll wind up just like him. Diseased!

WESLEY: *(dazed)* I'm hungry.

EMMA: You're sick! What're you doing with his clothes on? Are you supposed to be the head of the family now or something? The Big Cheese? Daddy Bear?

WESLEY: I tried his remedy, but it didn't work.

EMMA: He's got a remedy?

WESLEY: *(half to himself)* I tried taking a hot bath. Hot as I could stand it. Then freezing cold. Then walking around naked. But it didn't work. Nothing happened. I was waiting for something to happen. I went outside. I was freezing cold out there and I looked for something to put over me. I started digging around in the garbage and I found his clothes.

EMMA: Digging around in the garbage?

WESLEY: I had the lamb's blood dripping down my arms. I thought it was me for a second. I thought it was me bleeding.

EMMA: You're disgusting. You're even more disgusting than him. And that's pretty disgusting. *(looking at* ELLA, *still asleep)* What's she doing?

WESLEY: I started putting all his clothes on. His baseball cap, his tennis shoes, his overcoat. And every time I put one thing on it seemed like a part of him was growing on me. I could feel him taking over me.

EMMA: *(crossing up to table, tapping crop on her leg)* What is she, asleep or something? *(she whacks* ELLA *across the butt with the riding crop)* WAKE UP! (ELLA *stays sleeping)*

WESLEY: I could feel myself retreating. I could feel him coming in and me going out. Just like the change of the guards.

EMMA: Well, don't eat your heart out about it. You did the best you could.

WESLEY: I didn't do a thing.

EMMA: That's what I mean.

WESLEY: I just grew up here.

EMMA: *(crossing down to* WESLEY*)* Have you got any money?

WESLEY starts digging around in the pockets of the overcoat.

EMMA: What're you fishing around in there for? That's *his* coat.

WESLEY: I thought you were supposed to be in jail?

EMMA: *(crossing back up to table)* I was.

WESLEY: What happened?

EMMA: *(picking up* ELLA's *handbag and going through it)* I used my in-genuity. I made use of my innate criminal intelligence.

EMMA throws things onto the floor from ELLA's *pocket book as she searches through it.*

WESLEY: What'd you do?

EMMA: I got out.

WESLEY: I know, but how?

EMMA: I made sexual overtures to the sergeant. That's how. Easy.

She takes a big wad of money out of pocket book and a set of car keys, then throws the bag away. She holds up the money.

EMMA: I'm going into crime. It's the only thing that pays these days.

WESLEY: *(looking at roll of bills in* EMMA's *hand)* Where'd she get that?

EMMA: Where do you think?

WESLEY: You're taking her car?

EMMA: It's the perfect self-employment. Crime. No credentials. No di-plomas. No overhead. No upkeep. Just straight profit. Right off the top.

WESLEY: How come I'm going backwards?

EMMA: *(moving in toward* WESLEY*)* Because you don't look ahead. That's why. You don't see the writing on the wall. You gotta learn how to read these things, Wes. It's deadly otherwise. You can't be-lieve people when they look you in the eyes. You gotta' look be-hind them. See what they're standing in front of. What they're hid-ing. Everybody's hiding, Wes. Everybody. Nobody looks like what they are.

WESLEY: What are you?

EMMA: *(moving away)* I'm gone. I'm gone! Never to return.

ELLA suddenly wakes up on the table. She sits up straight.

ELLA: *(as though waking from a bad dream)* EMMA!!

EMMA *looks at her, then runs off stage left.* ELLA *sits there on table staring in horror at* WESLEY. *She doesn't recognize him.*

ELLA: *(to* WESLEY*)* Weston! Was that Emma?

WESLEY: It's me, Mom.

ELLA: *(yelling off stage but still on table)* EMMA!! *(she jumps off table and looks for a coat)* We've got to catch her! She can't run off like that! That horse will kill her! Where's my coat? *(to* WESLEY*)* WHERE'S MY COAT?

WESLEY: You weren't wearing one.

ELLA: *(to* WESLEY*)* Go catch her, Weston! She's your daughter! She's trying to run away!

WESLEY: Let her go.

ELLA: I can't let her go! I'm responsible!

Huge explosion off stage. Flash of light, then silence. WESLEY *and* ELLA *just stand there staring.* EMERSON *enters from right, giggling. He's a small man in a suit.*

EMERSON: Jeeezus! Did you ever hear a thing like that? What a wallop! Jeezus Christ! *(giggles)*

WESLEY *and* ELLA *look at him.*

EMERSON: Old Slater musta' packed it brim full. I never heard such a godalmighty bang in my whole career.

SLATER, *his partner, enters from right, holding out the skinned lamb carcass. He's taller than* EMERSON, *also in a suit. They both giggle as though they'd pulled off a halloween stunt.*

SLATER: Emerson, get a load a'this! *(giggling)* Did you see this thing? *(to* WESLEY*)* What is this, a skinned goat?

WESLEY: *(blank)* Lamb.

SLATER: Oh, it's a lamb! *(they laugh)* Looks like somebody's afterbirth to me! *(they laugh hysterically)*

WESLEY: What was that bang?

They stop laughing and look at WESLEY. *They laugh again, then stop.*

EMERSON: Bang? What bang?

WESLEY: That explosion.

EMERSON: Oh that! That was just a little reminder. A kind of a post-hypnotic suggestion. *(they laugh)*

ELLA: Who are these men, Weston?

EMERSON: *(to* WESLEY*)* Weston? You're Weston?

WESLEY: My father.

EMERSON: *(to SLATER)* Looks a little young, don't ya' think?

SLATER: *(dropping lamb carcass into fence enclosure)* Well, if she says he's Weston, he must be Weston.

ELLA: What are these men doing here? *(she moves away from them)*

EMERSON: *(to WESLEY)* So you're Weston? We had a different picture in mind. We had someone altogether different in mind.

WESLEY: What was it that blew up out there?

EMERSON: Something that wasn't paid for. Something past due.

SLATER: Long overdue.

WESLEY: The car. You blew up the car.

EMERSON: Bingo!

They crack up. WESLEY *moves upstage and looks out as though trying to see outside.*

ELLA: Get these men out of here, Weston! They're in my kitchen.

SLATER: *(looking around)* Some mess in here, boy. I couldn't live like this if you paid me.

EMERSON: Well, that's what comes from not paying your bills. You let one thing slide; first thing you know you let everything slide. You let everything go downhill until you wind up in a dungheap like this.

WESLEY: *(looking out, upstage)* There's a fire out there.

SLATER: It'll go out. It's just a gelignite-nitro mixture. Doesn't burn for long. May leave a few scars on the lawn but nothin' permanent.

WESLEY: *(without emotion, still looking out)* Nothing left of the car.

SLATER: That's right. Very thorough. The Irish developed it. Beautiful stuff. Never know what hit ya'.

EMERSON: *(to WESLEY)* Well, we gotta' run, Weston. But you can get the general drift. *(they start to leave; EMERSON stops)* Oh, and if you see your old man, you might pass on the info. We hate to keep repeating ourselves. The first time is great, but after that it gets pretty boring.

SLATER: *(to WESLEY)* Don't forget to give that lamb some milk. He looks pretty bad off.

They both laugh loudly, then exit. ELLA *is facing downstage now, staring at the lamb carcass in the pen.* WESLEY *has his back to her upstage. He looks out. Pause.*

ELLA: *(staring at dead lamb)* I must've slept right through the day. How long did I sleep?

They stay in these positions facing away from each other.

WESLEY: Not so long.

ELLA: And Emma left. She really left on that horse. I didn't think she'd do it. I had a dream she was leaving. That's what woke me up.

WESLEY: She was right here in the kitchen.

ELLA: I must've slept right through it. *(pause, as she stares at lamb carcass)* Oh! You know what, Wes?

WESLEY: What?

ELLA: Something just went right through me. Just from looking at this lamb.

WESLEY: What?

ELLA: That story your father used to tell about that eagle. You remember that?

WESLEY: Yeah.

ELLA: You remember the whole thing?

WESLEY: Yeah.

ELLA: I don't. I remember something about it. But it just went right through me.

WESLEY: Oh.

ELLA: *(after pause)* I remember he keeps coming back and swooping down on the shed roof and then flying off.

WESLEY: Yeah.

ELLA: What else?

WESLEY: I don't know.

ELLA: You remember. What happens next?

WESLEY: A cat comes.

ELLA: That's right. A big tom cat comes. Right out in the fields. And he jumps up on top of that roof to sniff around in all the entrails or whatever it was.

WESLEY: *(still with back to her)* And that eagle comes down and picks up the cat in his talons and carries him screaming off into the sky.

ELLA: *(staring at lamb)* That's right. And they fight. They fight like crazy in the middle of the sky. The cat's tearing his chest out, and the eagle's trying to drop him, but the cat won't let go because he knows if he falls he'll die.

WESLEY: And the eagle's being torn apart in midair. The eagle's trying to free himself from the cat, and the cat won't let go.

ELLA: And they come crashing down to the earth. Both of them come crashing down. Like one whole thing.

They stay like that with WESLEY *looking off upstage, his back to* ELLA, *and* ELLA *downstage, looking at the lamb. Lights fade very slowly to black.*

CURTAIN

PROPERTY PLOT

ACT ONE

On Stage

Breakfast table, with red oilcloth cover
Plates, cups, silverware
Mismatched metal chairs (4)
Two pairs of ruffled, red-checked curtains, suspended in mid-air
Refrigerator, with bacon and bread
Small gas stove, with frying pan in drawer
Pile of wooden debris and torn screen (remains of broken door)
Wheelbarrow

Off Stage

Alarm clock
Hand-painted charts, which show correct way to cut up a frying chicken
Rope halter
Briefcase
Collapsible fence structure (for lamb)
Lamb (live)
Large duffel bag, full of dirty laundry
Large bag of artichokes

ACT TWO

On Stage

Material for new door
Hammers, nails, saw, wood, sawdust
Pot of artichokes, on stove
Sheets of cardboard
Magic markers
Tape measure

Off Stage

Bag of groceries
Two wads of money
Deed
Briefcase, with legal document

On Stage

    Fence enclosure, with live lamb
    Pot of coffee, on stove
    Pile of clean laundry
    Food, in refrigerator, including ham and eggs
    Plates, cups, silverware

Off Stage

    Riding crop
    Handbag, with wad of money and car keys
    Skinned lamb carcass

NEW PLAYS

★ **MONTHS ON END by Craig Pospisil.** In comic scenes, one for each month of the year, we follow the intertwined worlds of a circle of friends and family whose lives are poised between happiness and heartbreak. "...a triumph...these twelve vignettes all form crucial pieces in the eternal puzzle known as human relationships, an area in which the playwright displays an assured knowledge that spans deep sorrow to unbounded happiness." *–Ann Arbor News.* "...rings with emotional truth, humor...[an] endearing contemplation on love...entertaining and satisfying." *–Oakland Press.* [5M, 5W] ISBN: 0-8222-1892-5

★ **GOOD THING by Jessica Goldberg.** Brings us into the households of John and Nancy Roy, forty-something high-school guidance counselors whose marriage has been increasingly on the rocks and Dean and Mary, recent graduates struggling to make their way in life. "...a blend of gritty social drama, poetic humor and unsubtle existential contemplation..." *–Variety.* [3M, 3W] ISBN: 0-8222-1869-0

★ **THE DEAD EYE BOY by Angus MacLachlan.** Having fallen in love at their Narcotics Anonymous meeting, Billy and Shirley-Diane are striving to overcome the past together. But their relationship is complicated by the presence of Sorin, Shirley-Diane's fourteen-year-old son, a damaged reminder of her dark past. "...a grim, insightful portrait of an unmoored family..." *–NY Times.* "MacLachlan's play isn't for the squeamish, but then, tragic stories delivered at such an unrelenting fever pitch rarely are." *–Variety.* [1M, 1W, 1 boy] ISBN: 0-8222-1844-5

★ **[SIC] by Melissa James Gibson.** In adjacent apartments three young, ambitious neighbors come together to discuss, flirt, argue, share their dreams and plan their futures with unequal degrees of deep hopefulness and abject despair. "A work...concerned with the sound and power of language..." *–NY Times.* "...a wonderfully original take on urban friendship and the comedy of manners—a *Design for Living* for our times..." *–NY Observer.* [3M, 2W] ISBN: 0-8222-1872-0

★ **LOOKING FOR NORMAL by Jane Anderson.** Roy and Irma's twenty-five-year marriage is thrown into turmoil when Roy confesses that he is actually a woman trapped in a man's body, forcing the couple to wrestle with the meaning of their marriage and the delicate dynamics of family. "Jane Anderson's bittersweet transgender domestic comedy-drama ...is thoughtful and touching and full of wit and wisdom. A real audience pleaser." *–Hollywood Reporter.* [5M, 4W] ISBN: 0-8222-1857-7

★ **ENDPAPERS by Thomas McCormack.** The regal Joshua Maynard, the old and ailing head of a mid-sized, family-owned book-publishing house in New York City, must name a successor. One faction in the house backs a smart, "pragmatic" manager, the other faction a smart, "sensitive" editor and both factions fear what the other's man could do to this house— and to them. "If Kaufman and Hart had undertaken a comedy about the publishing business, they might have written *Endpapers*...a breathlessly fast, funny, and thoughtful comedy ...keeps you amused, guessing, and often surprised...profound in its empathy for the paradoxes of human nature." *–NY Magazine.* [7M, 4W] ISBN: 0-8222-1908-5

★ **THE PAVILION by Craig Wright.** By turns poetic and comic, romantic and philosophical, this play asks old lovers to face the consequences of difficult choices made long ago. "The script's greatest strength lies in the genuineness of its feeling." *–Houston Chronicle.* "Wright's perceptive, gently witty writing makes this familiar situation fresh and thoroughly involving." *–Philadelphia Inquirer.* [2M, 1W (flexible casting)] ISBN: 0-8222-1898-4

DRAMATISTS PLAY SERVICE, INC.
440 Park Avenue South, New York, NY 10016 212-683-8960 Fax 212-213-1539
postmaster@dramatists.com www.dramatists.com

NEW PLAYS

★ **BE AGGRESSIVE by Annie Weisman.** Vista Del Sol is paradise, sandy beaches, avocado-lined streets. But for seventeen-year-old cheerleader Laura, everything changes when her mother is killed in a car crash, and she embarks on a journey to the Spirit Institute of the South where she can learn "cheer" with Bible belt intensity. "...filled with lingual gymnastics...stylized rapid-fire dialogue..." *–Variety.* "...a new, exciting, and unique voice in the American theatre..." *–BackStage West.* [1M, 4W, extras] ISBN: 0-8222-1894-1

★ **FOUR by Christopher Shinn.** Four people struggle desperately to connect in this quiet, sophisticated, moving drama. "...smart, broken-hearted...Mr. Shinn has a precocious and forgiving sense of how power shifts in the game of sexual pursuit...He promises to be a playwright to reckon with..." *–NY Times.* "A voice emerges from an American place. It's got humor, sadness and a fresh and touching rhythm that tell of the loneliness and secrets of life...[a] poetic, haunting play." *–NY Post.* [3M, 1W] ISBN: 0-8222-1850-X

★ **WONDER OF THE WORLD by David Lindsay-Abaire.** A madcap picaresque involving Niagara Falls, a lonely tour-boat captain, a pair of bickering private detectives and a husband's dirty little secret. "Exceedingly whimsical and playfully wicked. Winning and genial. A top-drawer production." *–NY Times.* "Full frontal lunacy is on display. A most assuredly fresh and hilarious tragicomedy of marital discord run amok...absolutely hysterical..." *–Variety.* [3M, 4W (doubling)] ISBN: 0-8222-1863-1

★ **QED by Peter Parnell.** Nobel Prize-winning physicist and all-around genius Richard Feynman holds forth with captivating wit and wisdom in this fascinating biographical play that originally starred Alan Alda. "QED is a seductive mix of science, human affections, moral courage, and comic eccentricity. It reflects on, among other things, death, the absence of God, travel to an unexplored country, the pleasures of drumming, and the need to know and understand." *–NY Magazine.* "Its rhythms correspond to the way that people—even geniuses—approach and avoid highly emotional issues, and it portrays Feynman with affection and awe." *–The New Yorker.* [1M, 1W] ISBN: 0-8222-1924-7

★ **UNWRAP YOUR CANDY by Doug Wright.** Alternately chilling and hilarious, this deliciously macabre collection of four bedtime tales for adults is guaranteed to keep you awake for nights on end. "Engaging and intellectually satisfying...a treat to watch." *–NY Times.* "Fiendishly clever. Mordantly funny and chilling. Doug Wright teases, freezes and zaps us." *–Village Voice.* "Four bite-size plays that bite back." *–Variety.* [flexible casting] ISBN: 0-8222-1871-2

★ **FURTHER THAN THE FURTHEST THING by Zinnie Harris.** On a remote island in the middle of the Atlantic secrets are buried. When the outside world comes calling, the islanders find their world blown apart from the inside as well as beyond. "Harris winningly produces an intimate and poetic, as well as political, family saga." *–Independent (London).* "Harris' enthralling adventure of a play marks a departure from stale, well-furrowed theatrical terrain." *–Evening Standard (London).* [3M, 2W] ISBN: 0-8222-1874-7

★ **THE DESIGNATED MOURNER by Wallace Shawn.** The story of three people living in a country where what sort of books people like to read and how they choose to amuse themselves becomes both firmly personal and unexpectedly entangled with questions of survival. "This is a playwright who does not just tell you what it is like to be arrested at night by goons or to fall morally apart and become an aimless yet weirdly contented ghost yourself. He has the originality to make you feel it." *–Times (London).* "A fascinating play with beautiful passages of writing..." *–Variety.* [2M, 1W] ISBN: 0-8222-1848-8

DRAMATISTS PLAY SERVICE, INC.
440 Park Avenue South, New York, NY 10016 212-683-8960 Fax 212-213-1539
postmaster@dramatists.com www.dramatists.com

NEW PLAYS

★ **SHEL'S SHORTS by Shel Silverstein.** Lauded poet, songwriter and author of children's books, the incomparable Shel Silverstein's short plays are deeply infused with the same wicked sense of humor that made him famous. "…[a] childlike honesty and twisted sense of humor." –*Boston Herald*. "…terse dialogue and an absurdity laced with a tang of dread give [*Shel's Shorts*] more than a trace of Samuel Beckett's comic existentialism." –*Boston Phoenix*. [flexible casting] ISBN: 0-8222-1897-6

★ **AN ADULT EVENING OF SHEL SILVERSTEIN by Shel Silverstein.** Welcome to the darkly comic world of Shel Silverstein, a world where nothing is as it seems and where the most innocent conversation can turn menacing in an instant. These ten imaginative plays vary widely in content, but the style is unmistakable. "…[*An Adult Evening*] shows off Silverstein's virtuosic gift for wordplay…[and] sends the audience out…with a clear appreciation of human nature as perverse and laughable." –*NY Times*. [flexible casting] ISBN: 0-8222-1873-9

★ **WHERE'S MY MONEY? by John Patrick Shanley.** A caustic and sardonic vivisection of the institution of marriage, laced with the author's inimitable razor-sharp wit. "…Shanley's gift for acid-laced one-liners and emotionally tumescent exchanges is certainly potent…" –*Variety*. "…lively, smart, occasionally scary and rich in reverse wisdom." –*NY Times*. [3M, 3W] ISBN: 0-8222-1865-8

★ **A FEW STOUT INDIVIDUALS by John Guare.** A wonderfully screwy comedy-drama that figures Ulysses S. Grant in the throes of writing his memoirs, surrounded by a cast of fantastical characters, including the Emperor and Empress of Japan, the opera star Adelina Patti and Mark Twain. "Guare's smarts, passion and creativity skyrocket to awesome heights…" –*Star Ledger*. "…precisely the kind of good new play that you might call an everyday miracle…every minute of it is fresh and newly alive…" –*Village Voice*. [10M, 3W] ISBN: 0-8222-1907-7

★ **BREATH, BOOM by Kia Corthron.** A look at fourteen years in the life of Prix, a Bronx native, from her ruthless girl-gang leadership at sixteen through her coming to maturity at thirty. "…vivid world, believable and eye-opening, a place worthy of a dramatic visit, where no one would want to live but many have to." –*NY Times*. "…rich with humor, terse vernacular strength and gritty detail…" –*Variety*. [1M, 9W] ISBN: 0-8222-1849-6

★ **THE LATE HENRY MOSS by Sam Shepard.** Two antagonistic brothers, Ray and Earl, are brought together after their father, Henry Moss, is found dead in his seedy New Mexico home in this classic Shepard tale. "…His singular gift has been for building mysteries out of the ordinary ingredients of American family life…" –*NY Times*. "…rich moments …Shepard finds gold." –*LA Times*. [7M, 1W] ISBN: 0-8222-1858-5

★ **THE CARPETBAGGER'S CHILDREN by Horton Foote.** One family's history spanning from the Civil War to WWII is recounted by three sisters in evocative, intertwining monologues. "…bittersweet music—[a] rhapsody of ambivalence…in its modest, garrulous way…theatrically daring." –*The New Yorker*. [3W] ISBN: 0-8222-1843-7

★ **THE NINA VARIATIONS by Steven Dietz.** In this funny, fierce and heartbreaking homage to *The Seagull*, Dietz puts Chekhov's star-crossed lovers in a room and doesn't let them out. "A perfect little jewel of a play…" –*Shepherdstown Chronicle*. "…a delightful revelation of a writer at play; and also an odd, haunting, moving theater piece of lingering beauty." –*Eastside Journal (Seattle)*. [1M, 1W (flexible casting)] ISBN: 0-8222-1891-7

DRAMATISTS PLAY SERVICE, INC.
440 Park Avenue South, New York, NY 10016 212-683-8960 Fax 212-213-1539
postmaster@dramatists.com   www.dramatists.com